CROCODILES

· ·

OF AUSTRALIA

Grahame Webb and Charlie Manolis

T0342715

NEW
HOLLAND

First published in 2009 by New Holland Publishers
Sydney

Level 1, 178 Fox Valley Road, Wahroonga, NSW 2076, Australia

newhollandpublishers.com

A record of this book is held at the National Library of Australia.

ISBN 9781741108484

Managing Director: Fiona Schultz
Senior project editor: Joanna Tovia
Editor: Anne Savage
Proofreader: Carolyn Beaumont
Design: Hayley Norman
Production Director: Arlene Gippert
Printed in China

10 9 8 7 6 5 4 3 2

Keep up with New Holland Publishers:

 NewHollandPublishers
 @newhollandpublishers

Photographic Acknowledgements

Photographic positions: t = top, b = bottom, i = inset, l = left, r = right

All photographs by Grahame Webb with the exception of the following:

Tom Dacey: p. 5t, 9b, 14b, 22t; Fred Grahl: p. 12b; Jim Frazier: p. 57t; Ted Jackson: p. 9t, 45b; Garry Lindner: p. 96-97, 99rt; Family of Curly Bardkadubbu, courtesy of Museum and Art Gallery of the Northern Territory (Kumoken – The Crocodile): p. 13t, 90b; The Northern Territory News: p. 13t, 90b; John Pomeroy: p. 104lb; Mark West: p. 97i, 98rt, 104lt.

Acknowledgements

Much of the information reported in this book has been gained from working on crocodiles for more than three decades, usually with teams of individuals, often volunteers seeking the experience, but including the hundreds of researchers with whom we have collaborated over the years. Our own staff members from Crocodylus Park have always been ready to do that little bit more than can reasonably be expected, to learn more about crocodiles, and it helps make a book like this possible. Foremost amongst those who have helped and encouraged us, and been tolerant of the long hours away from home, are our spouses and children. For them, crocodiles have become part of their daily lives, whether they wished it upon themselves or not, and we recognise the debt of gratitude they deserve. We seem to know a great deal more about crocodiles now than we did in the 1970s, but much remains unknown—there are plenty of questions for future generations to address.

Dedication

For those who have shared our ride with crocodiles

CONTENTS

An Introduction to Crocodiles

Saltwater Crocodile

*C*rocodiles are an easily recognised group of reptiles which share with lizards, snakes and turtles a dry scaly skin, reproduction by yolk-laden eggs (which in some cases develop inside the female's body), and *ectothermy* or cold-bloodedness, in which body temperatures change with environmental temperatures rather than being constant as in most mammals and birds. There are only two crocodile species in Australia, the Saltwater Crocodile or 'saltie' (*Crocodylus porosus*), also called the Estuarine or Indo-Pacific Crocodile, and the Australian Freshwater Crocodile or 'freshie' (*Crocodylus johnstoni*), also called the Johnston's River Crocodile. They are found in the tropical north because they need warm, wet conditions to survive. Crocodiles are almost exclusively carnivorous, preying on animals ranging from small insects and shrimps to cattle, horses and buffalo.

Crocodiles take us back to when our primitive ancestors had to contend with them whenever they went near water. But crocodiles go back much further. Crocodiles are essentially identical to the ones that were alive with the dinosaurs, to which they are closely related, up to 200 million years ago. Much of the secret lives of crocodiles has been painstakingly unravelled over the past four decades, but there is still more to learn and understand.

Freshwater Crocodile

How do Crocodiles Hunt?

*C*rocodiles are specialist hunters which have mastered a niche existence, that of a water's edge predator, perhaps more successfully than any other living animal. From the safety and security of the water they move stealthily next to the bank, making hardly a ripple. Here they sit patiently in the shallows, their feet on the bottom in sand or mud, waiting for small aquatic animals—crabs, crayfish, prawns, fish, turtles—to come close enough so they can strike sideways into the water and catch them. Often they swing tail and head inward at the same time, to both trap and grasp their prey. From the same 'sit and wait' position, they can launch themselves at terrestrial animals coming to the water.

The Hunter's Periscope

The way in which a crocodile operates is similar to a submarine. The large bulk of the submarine is often hidden from view below the water, but the periscope, laden with sensing devices, can extend above the surface to provide information on the best course to take. With just the top of the crocodile's head (the 'periscope') above the surface, it can see, hear, smell and breathe while the bulk of its body is hidden. A crocodile can reorient its body without creating surface ripples if it senses prey near the water's edge. Then it submerges and moves closer, sometimes raising the 'periscope' a second time to check on position. The prey animal at best may see only the 'periscope', unaware of the large body mass beneath the water being positioned for attack.

Even in clear water, the real size of an approaching crocodile is distorted

How do Freshies and Salties Differ?

*T*he main and obvious differences are the width of the snout between the eyes and the nostrils, and the height of the eyes above the base of the snout. Freshwater Crocodiles have a thin, narrow snout, with the eyes set reasonably high. Saltwater Crocodiles have a broader, chunkier snout, with the eyes tending to be lower set. In both species the snout becomes more robust with increasing size and age. Freshwater Crocodiles strike at small prey very fast, often pinning them at the tip of the narrow snout and lifting them out of the water, like chopsticks picking up a peanut, and killing by working them back to the crushing teeth in the back of the jaw. Saltwater Crocodiles strike with a more determined blow, like huge pliers, crushing small prey or getting a firm grip on larger prey to prepare for the ensuing struggle. Crocodile snout shape tells us much about foods and feeding etiquette. Another distinguishing feature is the extent of bony armour on the body. Freshwater Crocodiles have an additional row of enlarged bone plates between the neck and the head, the *postoccipital scutes*.

Are Alligators Similar to Crocodiles?

Alligators have broad snouts

*C*rocodiles and alligators are very similar in many ways, and their lifestyles are almost identical. Alligators have a broader, more shovel-shaped snout than crocodiles, and the teeth of the lower jaw fit into sockets within the edge of the broad upper jaw. The enlarged 4th tooth from the front, on the lower jaw, is hidden when an alligator's jaws are closed. In crocodiles' narrower snouts, the teeth of the bottom jaw are exposed along the side of the top jaw, and the large 4th tooth on the lower jaw is fully exposed in a notch when the jaws are closed. Otherwise, the jaws and teeth work in an identical manner.

Rarely sighted, this 5.5m long Saltwater Crocodile is one of the biggest ever photographed

How Big can Crocodiles Grow?

*S*altwater Crocodiles are generally regarded as the largest living crocodile, indeed, the largest living reptile and the closest link to the giant reptiles known from the fossil record. Some Saltwater Crocodiles have been measured definitively at 6.1m long, and weighing about 1 tonne. The largest crocodiles are like the people who exceed 2.1m in height—rare individuals that grew faster and bigger than normal.

Male Saltwater Crocodiles typically cease growing at 4.3–4.9m, no matter how long they live

Have Crocodiles Existed for Long?

*T*oday's crocodilians are often referred to as living fossils, but this is only partly true. The earliest crocodilians appeared around 200 million years ago. Most became extinct with the dinosaurs, 65 million years ago. The few survivors, which included Eusuchian crocodiles, the ancestors of the three living groups, separated from each other 60+ million years ago.

How Did They Survive Extinction?

*W*e will never know for sure why some crocodiles survived when so many crocodiles and other large reptiles became extinct 65 million years ago. Given that dramatic environmental changes interfering with the sun's ability to heat the atmosphere almost certainly occurred, it is also a given that many reptiles would not have been able to regulate body temperature at the levels needed for survival.

If the sun was obscured so that the crocodiles could not bask, perhaps some of them used warm geothermal springs for thermoregulation.

As carrion eaters, food in the form of dead and dying reptiles was probably abundant for those crocodiles that could maintain their body temperature. Crocodiles can grow in the dark if sufficient vitamins are available in their food.

Interestingly, adult female crocodiles can 'wait out' adverse conditions for long periods. In the US, a captive Chinese Alligator housed in inadequate environments had not bred for up to 50 years, but retained the ability to breed, and did so, when the right environmental conditions were provided. It suggests that the ancestors of today's crocodiles could have lived through an environmental catastrophe for at least 50 years, breeding and multiplying when conditions changed.

> There are 23 species of living crocodilians around the world, divided into three distinct groups: true crocodiles; alligators and caimans; and gharials and false gharials. The three major groups appear to have been separated from each other for at least 60 million years.

Do Aboriginal People Fear Crocodiles?

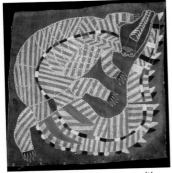

Aboriginal art often features crocodiles

*H*umans have always had to contend with crocodiles. Crocodiles and their eggs were a source of food for people, but people were a source of food for crocodiles as well. That humanity has always had to take crocodilians seriously is reflected in the stories, songs, legends, artwork and culture of many peoples. Nowhere is this more apparent than in Aboriginal culture in northern Australia. Crocodiles are involved in Creation stories, songs and dances, have long featured prominently in rock and bark paintings, and have significant 'Dreaming' sites linked with them. The spirits of certain deceased people are believed to reside in some large crocodiles, and the deaths of these crocodiles are associated with wailing for the lost spirits. Crocodiles also featured in ancient Egyptian beliefs, and mummified Nile Crocodiles were entombed with pharaohs.

Crocodiles have always been a source of food for Aboriginal people

Is Crocodile Hunting Illegal?

Crocodile skin makes fashionable leather goods

Crocodile skins have been used for leather goods since at least the 1800s, but it was not until the 1900s that the aesthetics of the scale pattern became important in the fashion industry. This stimulated commercial hunting in many countries. Demand increased dramatically after World War II, and wild populations of many crocodile species plummeted. At the time few people really cared about dangerous 'pests', and the same treatment was being directed at lions, tigers and other predators.

It was not until the 1960s that conservationists began to champion the cause of crocodiles. In Australia, Saltwater and Freshwater Crocodiles were both protected at State and Territory levels throughout their range, between 1964 and 1974. In 1972 the Commonwealth Government imposed an export ban on crocodile skins that essentially stopped the trade in Queensland, the last state to enact protection. Internationally, the Convention on International Trade in Endangered Species of Wild Fauna and Flora (CITES) came into force in 1975, with all living crocodilian species listed on its appendices. This restricted international trade in wild crocodiles but allowed ongoing trade in captive-bred animals.

Legal but unregulated hunting depleted crocodile populations

Deliberately attracting crocodiles to a boat can be dangerous

Have Crocodile Numbers Recovered?

*I*n Australia, wild populations brought to the brink of extinction through 20–30 years of unrestricted commercial hunting were given a chance to recover once they were protected by law. They rebounded in numbers, firstly with annual cohorts of baby crocodiles getting bigger each year, and spreading further and further. The public had agreed to protect crocodiles when few were left, but started to question the wisdom of that decision in the early 1980s when Saltwater Crocodiles were once again abundant and starting to prey on people and domestic stock. To turn public resentment to public support, the Northern Territory pioneered sustainable crocodile use, a type of management that allowed some crocodiles to be used commercially, creating tangible incentives for landowners and the community to tolerate them, which in turn was hoped would engender public support for the populations to continue expanding. Full recovery of wild Saltwater Crocodile populations has taken place in the Northern Territory and the species' future is both sound and secure, something rarely achieved in the conservation of large and serious predators.

Is Conservation Under Threat?

*T*he most serious long-term threat to crocodile conservation globally is the steady loss of wetland habitats to alternative land uses, especially agriculture and aquaculture. In northern Australia, our mangroves, forests and wetlands are in remarkably good shape, and poverty is not driving habitat loss. But this is not the case in many countries. Wetlands loss is usually associated with a need to produce food and create economic wealth, but there is a serious wildlife conservation price to pay. Crocodiles are frequently seen negatively, as an economic burden for the people, often in poverty, sharing their lives with them. This creates political and humanitarian dilemmas for governments, which are expected to look after both people and wildlife.

Many countries are finding new ways to encourage people to value crocodiles positively, promoting conservation within and outside protected areas, but it is a challenge, and it is rarely successful across a species' range.

Populations in northern Australia have recovered

The loss of wetland habitats is the most serious threat to crocodiles

Will Climate Change Have an Impact?

*T*he current increase in global temperatures has stimulated interest in how a great many wild species and habitats will respond. One point of vulnerability for the Australian Freshwater Crocodile lies in the way its reproductive strategy is adapted to the prevailing weather pattern. There are only a few weeks in the year when this species can nest successfully. If they nest too early, ground temperatures are too low to allow successful embryological development; if they nest too late, the nests are inundated by wet-season rains. If climate change reduces the extent of the warm dry season (August–November) in northern Australia, the window for success will close and the species will become extinct.

With the Saltwater Crocodile, which has a longer wet-season nesting period (November–May), climate change is unlikely to close the window completely, but may well affect success in marginal areas. For example, across the Kimberley coast in Western Australia nest temperatures are very high now, giving a bias in sex ratios towards females and high embryonic mortality due to overheating.

Any significant rises in sea level, or prolongation of the dry season, could be expected to alter the wetland habitats occupied by both species, but in largely unpredictable ways.

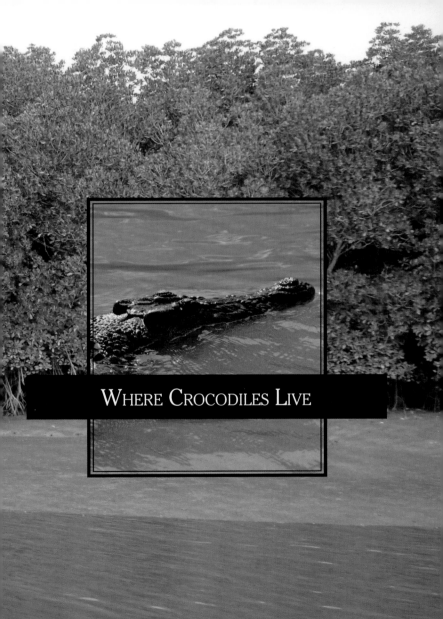

WHERE CROCODILES LIVE

Temperature is one of the main factors restricting crocodiles to northern Australia

Why do Crocodiles Live Up North?

*C*rocodiles extend from around Broome in the northwest of Western Australia, across the Kimberley to the Northern Territory, through the Gulf of Carpentaria to Cape York and the Torres Strait, and down the east coast of Queensland to Rockhampton. Saltwater Crocodiles occupy the coast and offshore islands, tidal rivers and coastal swamps, both freshwater and saline, and sometimes extend into the freshwater upper reaches of rivers. Freshwater Crocodiles tend to be restricted to the inland rivers and billabongs, occasionally extending down to saline tidal wetlands, but rarely reaching the coast. Northern Australia has a climate characterised by the name 'wet-dry tropics'. Most of the rain, which can exceed 2m per year, occurs in a distinct wet season from November to April. In some parts of the range, there is virtually no rain at all in the dry season (May–October). Every aspect of a crocodile's lifestyle seems adapted to the alternating wet and dry seasons.

Crocodiles are most abundant and productive in the Top End of the Northern Territory and across to the Weipa area of Cape York, where annual average maximum monthly temperatures are 32–33°C, minimums 22–24°C, and rainfall 1.4 to 1.8m per year; few months of the year have average minimums below 20°C.

What's in a Name?

*T*he names Saltwater Crocodile and Freshwater Crocodile are generalisations rather than precise definitions of where the two species live. Freshwater Crocodiles do indeed live mostly in the freshwater rivers, creeks, streams, billabongs, dams and swamps, well upstream of both tidal influence and saline water. But in some river systems they extend downstream into tidal and saline waters, where they live in uneasy harmony with their cousins.

Saltwater Crocodiles occupy many completely freshwater rivers, creeks and swamps, with some of the densest populations living in heavily vegetated freshwater swamps with no tidal influence. They are equally at home in tidal rivers and creeks where, through evaporation, salinity in the dry season can be very high, exceeding salinity in the ocean. They regularly move out of the mouths of rivers and around the coast and occupy offshore islands. In highly saline areas, they will visit any available source of fresh water to drink such as beachside lagoons and springs, but they have glands in the tongue which can concentrate excess salt and pump it out. These glands are present but not as efficient in Freshwater Crocodiles, and seldom need to be used. It suggests that the common ancestor of both species—and perhaps all true crocodiles—may have been marine.

Saltwater Crocodiles at sea are mostly found inshore but can travel impressive distances offshore

Do Crocodiles Move Around?

Darwin is a city built amongst crocodile habitat

Saltwater Crocodiles are frequently found at sea, moving around the coast, making forays in and out of coastal rivers, or moving between offshore islands. They can make significant offshore movements, as evidenced by the occasional individual turning up on isolated islands well distanced from any known population. A Saltwater Crocodile that arrived on the eastern Caroline Islands in the Pacific had travelled a minimum of 1360km from the nearest population, and another that turned up on the Marshall Islands was around 2000km from the nearest population. Freshwater Crocodiles are rarely sighted at sea. The finding of a near-intact juvenile Freshie in the stomach contents of a large Great White Shark caught off the coast of Queensland remains an intriguing mystery.

How do They Use the Tide?

Saltwater Crocodiles are adept at using the tide, both at sea and in tidal rivers. They commonly use the high tide to lift themselves up onto the bank to bask or to seek out dead animals they can smell on the floodplain. In the horizontal plane, the incoming tide causes water to flow upstream, often at such a rate that a tidal bore occurs, which reverses itself on the outgoing tide. The crocodiles use the flow to move upstream and down, often with slow propulsion from undulations of the tail, using relatively little energy to move tens of kilometres.

Do Crocodiles Become Stranded?

*M*ost crocodiles, both Saltwater and Freshwater, inhabit areas of permanent water in the dry season. They may spread out into temporary waters during the wet season when the plains are flooded, but move back when the rains cease. If the dry season is particularly prolonged, they may become stranded when waterways dry up. Freshwater Crocodiles are adept at moving along river and creek beds to find deeper pools, but they sometimes take refuge in overhangs of the banks of drying pools, or in small caverns burrowed into the banks when they were under water and now dried out. Saltwater Crocodiles trapped on drying floodplains will bury themselves in shallow mud, often at the base of paperbark trees, before it dries. Here they aestivate, remaining in a comatose state until the rains come. Depending on the location's exposure to the sun, and the time they are trapped, some die through overheating and desiccation.

Crocodiles can become stranded when the dry season goes on longer than usual

Are Crocodiles Territorial?

Crocodiles have one or more core areas of activity

Our understanding of 'territoriality' in Australian crocodiles remains in its infancy, partly because the technologies needed to track their movements efficiently and effectively have only been recently developed. As a generality, adult male Saltwater Crocodiles living in tidal rivers are not restricted to small areas, but rather drift upstream and downstream through areas occupied by other adult males. They may have core areas of activity separated by 10–20km. Females that have attained the size and social status needed to nest tend to be far less mobile than males. Among Freshwater Crocodiles living in dry-season refuge pools, there is a tendency for a pool to hold one or two large, dominant males however, it is quite common to find that the dominant male in the same pool the next year is a different individual. How this occurs can now be clarified through satellite-tracking studies.

Where are the Crocodile Havens?

Particularly in the Northern Territory, where Freshwater and Saltwater Crocodiles are most abundant, there are some rivers and locations of special interest.

The Alligator Rivers

In terms of protected areas, one of the gems in Australia's crocodile crown is Kakadu National Park in the Northern Territory. Kakadu's 20,000km^2

Floodplains in Kakadu National Park

include the East Alligator, South Alligator, West Alligator and Wildman rivers, all tidal rivers extending from the coast across vast floodplains to the Arnhem Land escarpment. Scattered across the floodplains is a great diversity of freshwater swamps, lagoons and billabongs, containing an abundance of Saltwater Crocodiles. Freshwater Crocodiles occupy all the upstream areas. The total population of crocodiles within Kakadu is thought to be in the vicinity of 5000–6000, excluding hatchlings.

The Mary River

For Saltwater Crocodiles the Mary River, located on the western side of Kakadu, is unrivalled—it has the highest density of Saltwater Crocodiles in Australia and the world and a number of tourist operations give visitors the chance to see them. In the downstream part of the river, at a site called Shady Camp, the saline tidal river waters meet the freshwater non-tidal habitat at a man-made barrage that is a crossing point for Saltwater Crocodiles moving between the tidal and non-tidal sections. Often, more than 20 crocodiles are sighted here per kilometre. The exceptionally high density is due to abundant food, proximity to Kakadu where crocodiles may be moving in and out continually, and ready access to fresh water. In the non-tidal freshwater side of Shady Camp, and all through the Mary River, there are also large numbers of Freshwater Crocodiles.

The McKinlay River

The McKinlay River is an upstream tributary of the Mary River, some 110km southeast of Darwin. It is an ephemeral river that flows rapidly during the wet season, typically December to April, and dries to a series of pools of varying depth and size during the dry season. What makes the McKinlay River important is that during the dry season the pools are small enough to be manageable in terms of catching a high proportion of the Freshwater Crocodiles that reside in them, so the river was selected as the main site in which their biology was first subjected to detailed research. The research program was initiated in 1978 and continues today. Thousands of Freshwater Crocodiles have been caught in the river, marked, released and re-caught over the years, allowing natural history parameters such as growth rate, movement, population size structure, population age structure and survival rates to be estimated.

The McKinlay River was acquired by the Northern Territory Government as a protected area so that research could continue in the long term, even more important now that cane toads have colonised the area, causing increased mortality in both Freshwater Crocodiles and the varanid lizards which are the main predators on their eggs.

Dry season pool in the McKinlay River mainstream

Lake Argyle and Lake Kununurra

Dams are sensitive environmental issues, but the damming of the Ord River at Kununurra in the eastern Kimberly of Western Australia has created one of the most spectacular wildlife habitats in Australia, which currently contains more than 20,000 Freshwater

Freshwater Crocodile habitat in the Arnhem Land Plateau

Crocodiles. At some 60km long and 30km wide, the lakes are a permanent wetland in a region that receives little rain and previously had limited fresh water during the dry season. They provide water for irrigated agriculture and remarkable wildlife viewing through a number of local tourist operations.

Where are the Protected Areas?

*A*cross northern Australia there are many protected areas that contain crocodiles. Some are very large, such as Kakadu National Park in the Northern Territory (20,000km²), the Jardine River (3,800km²) and Lakefield (5,430km²) National Parks in Cape York Peninsula, Queensland, and the proposed Mary River National Park in the Northern Territory (1,200 km²). Others are much smaller. They may contain Saltwater Crocodiles, Freshwater Crocodiles, or both. The crocodiles' abundance in the protected areas depends on many factors, but in particular latitude, which affects prevailing temperature conditions, and topography, which dictates the form of the rivers.

Managing protected areas is often a challenge for the authorities because Saltwater Crocodiles in any density represent a significant risk to the unwary visitor.

CROCODILE BEHAVIOUR

How do Crocodiles Keep Warm?

*C*rocodiles are often described as being 'cold-blooded', 'poikilothermic' or 'ectothermic'—all essentially the same thing. Unlike mammals and birds, they do not generate metabolic heat to keep the body warm when they are cold, nor are they effective at reducing body temperature through evaporative cooling. They have no sweat glands, and evaporation from the roof of the mouth at best may cool the brain just a little. Crocodiles control their body temperature by behavioural means. To warm up, they bask in the sun or seek out areas of warm water and, to prevent overheating, they seek shade or cool water or bury themselves in mud. Body temperatures

in excess of 35–36°C are very uncomfortable for a crocodile, and if prolonged will cause death. Preferred body temperature is around 30–32°C. Some crocodilians, such as the Chinese Alligator and the American Alligator, can survive body temperatures down to 0°C for prolonged periods, but neither Saltwater nor Freshwater Crocodiles are so tolerant.

Body temperature is regulated by behaviour

Is Being Cold-Blooded an Advantage?

*T*he major advantage for a crocodile of being cold-blooded is that it does not need to eat vast amounts of food just to keep warm in cool conditions. A 300kg crocodile, in an environment where its body temperature can be 31°C in the day and down to 22°C at night, may only need 1–2kg of food per week to sustain itself. A 300kg warm-blooded mammal would need to eat 10 times that amount, mostly to keep warm.

Tricks of the Trade

A crocodile's behavioural regulation of body temperature can be managed with extraordinary precision. For example, female crocodiles carrying a clutch of eggs with the young embryos developing within the eggs, will regulate their body temperature quite precisely around 31°C, optimum for the development of the embryos. Sick crocodiles

Basking is needed to increase body temperature

seek out warmer spots to raise their body temperatures to around 33–34°C, thus undergoing a behavioural fever that presumably stimulates their immune system.

Why do Crocodiles Bask in the Sun?

N ot surprisingly, one of the most common crocodile behaviours is basking, splayed out on dry land in full sunlight, typically in spots sheltered from the wind. In the winter months, when air temperatures can fall close to 10°C, crocodiles spend the night in the water, which is warmer. When the sun rises, they climb up on the bank, often orienting themselves so the sun's rays fall on the back of the head, warming the brain first so their senses function efficiently while the larger body mass heats. In the hot summer months, crocodiles avoid the sun, tending to stay in the water which is usually cooler, buried in mud at the water's edge, or up on the banks in the shade under trees.

> There are large energetic advantages in being able to cool down at night rather than maintaining the same body temperature at all times.

The aquatic posture allows crocodiles to make a quick escape

What is the Aquatic Posture?

No matter how head shape may have been modified by evolution, a crocodilian's ability to rest just below the surface of the water, with only the nostrils, eyes, ears and cranial platform exposed, has not been compromised. This *aquatic posture*, with its low profile, allows breathing and sensing with only a small part of the body exposed. The low profile no doubt assists when approaching potential prey, but may also be a response to other crocodiles that may be a territorial threat. A crocodile with its head exposed in the aquatic posture usually has its body horizontal in the water with some of the bony osteoderms of the back exposed, and the tail moving gently from side to side. If threatened, without moving its head it rapidly drops its body into a more or less vertical position, with the webbed hind feet splayed out. From this position, by raising the feet in the water and moving the tail, the crocodile can slip underwater backwards, with hardly a ripple on the surface, straighten up and swim off.

Crocodiles less than 2m long can launch themselves out of the water more than half their body length, so that even the hind limbs, tucked against the tail, are fully exposed.

How do Crocodiles Walk on Land?

*O*ne of the most common forms of locomotion on land is the *high walk*. In this gait, the short but powerful hind limbs lift the pelvic area, which in a crocodile is the balance point between the heavy tail and the remainder of the body, off the ground. The front legs lift the head and chest, and the tail drags along the ground. In this position, the muscles of the tail and back are pulled tight, giving the body some rigidity.

The crocodile moves forward in a slow, almost mechanical, stilted motion. With the weight of the body held up in the air, the crocodile curves to the left while the right front leg is extended or repositioned to balance the weight, then curves to the right so the back left leg can be moved forward and repositioned to hold the weight.

High walking is a slow and laborious gait, especially for large crocodiles, and at best reaches about 2km per hour over short distances.

The high walk is slow and laborious

Freshwater Crocodiles gallop over obstacles

Can Crocodiles Really Gallop?

*F*reshwater Crocodiles have developed a true gallop. The back legs launch the body forward and the front legs extend to receive it as the back legs move forward again. Galloping, typically used for short bursts to reach water, is a bounding gait which allows the crocodile to overcome obstacles such as rocks and logs. Bound length and speed vary with the size of the animal. For example, a 1m crocodile has a bound length of 0.65m (65 per cent of total length) and an average velocity of 11.5km per hour. A 2m crocodile has a bound length of 1.34m (57 per cent of total length) and an average velocity of 15.9km per hour. Some species, including Saltwater Crocodiles, have never been observed to gallop.

Sliding Down a Slippery Slope

*I*n tidal rivers where the difference between high and low tide exceeds 5m and the banks are mainly soft mud, Saltwater Crocodiles have become toboggan specialists. Having positioned themselves to bask at high tide, at low tide they can find themselves 5m above the water and 20m away from it. Unable to high walk across the mud because their legs sink into it, they simply slide down to the water. If the bank is not steep enough, they essentially 'swim' through the mud, body and tail undulating, fore and hind feet digging in to help maintain momentum.

Why do Crocodiles Jump?

*S*ome crocodile species, including Saltwater Crocodiles, have become adept at leaping out of the water to catch prey in overhanging trees, or snatch low-flying insects, bats and birds out of the air. The propulsion comes from the tail, and the height to which they can jump depends on body length.

Are They Good at Climbing?

*N*either Saltwater nor Freshwater Crocodiles are particularly adept at climbing. Both can make their way up a reasonably steep riverbank if they need to, but it is a rather ungainly affair. They do not climb trees to attack prey from above. Smaller crocodiles will climb up on logs in the water if the slope is modest. Larger crocodiles are too heavy to climb much. Hatchling Freshwater Crocodiles appear to be much more adept at climbing than hatchling Saltwater Crocodiles. Kept in pens with concrete brick walls 1–1.2m high, they sometimes scale the walls and either escape or are found sitting on the top—but not hatchling Saltwater Crocodiles. A 1.2m chain mesh fence is normally sufficient to contain both species.

Crocodiles are far more agile in the water than they are on land

How do Crocodiles Communicate?

Snout lifting is a sign of submission

*C*rocodiles communicate using visual signals, sounds and chemicals. The visual signals tend to be subtle and partly aimed at avoiding conflict. One of the most common is 'snout-lifting', in which a crocodile being approached by another lifts its snout in the air as a message of submission: 'You win, my friend'. Courtship involves the much smaller females doing a lot of snout-lifting to ensure they are not perceived by males as a threat. Snout-lifting is sometimes associated with everting two glands under the chin which secrete a musky exudate known to stimulate other crocodiles. It is likely that these glands, and two similar ones in the walls of the cloaca, play a role in chemical communication and perhaps marking of territories, but this has not been well researched.

The common behaviour of 'gaping', lying on the water's edge with the head facing the water and the mouth wide open exposing the teeth and bright yellow palate and tongue, also serves as a social signal: 'I'm here'. Gaping has multiple purposes, being used to orient the back of the head to the sun to warm the brain during the day, but also occurring at night, when a crocodile resting on the bank is approached by another crocodile in the water.

Gaping is a common pose at the water's edge

What are the Signs of Aggression?

*A*nother series of behaviours used for communication are inherently aggressive and challenging. 'Head slapping' onto the water's surface sends a low-frequency signal through the water advertising a crocodile's claim to an area and warning newcomers. It is unclear whether the strength of the head slap, which relates to size, sends more information.

Vibrating the sides of the body sends a low-frequency sound through water

Crocodiles facing off to each other will 'inflate' their bodies, making them look bigger. They also engage in 'tail arching', which tightens the muscles down the back so that the head can be swung against a rigid body to deliver a strong blow to a rival — the arched tail itself being a signal of intent. Gaping, in the context of facing off, is a highly aggressive signal. A crocodile that is inflated, with its tail arched, can vibrate its sides to create a 'bubbling display', in which the water on each side vibrates and bubbles, sending a low-frequency sound through the water. Growling, which is a very low frequency but intense sound, is another aggressive display, sometimes advertising presence but at other times part of a face-off ritual.

What does a Nip on the Tail Mean?

*S*ome behaviours, such as 'tail biting', involve contact. In a billabong, large dominant Freshwater Crocodiles assume ownership of the deepest parts; if other crocodiles swim over their territory, they will come up from underwater and bite them on the tail. Bite and rake marks on the tail, testimony to these interactions, are among the most common injuries in wild Freshwater Crocodiles.

Aggressive combat can lead to serious injury

Do Crocodiles Fight to the Death?

*A*lthough many crocodile communication behaviours involve ritualised, often aggressive signals, interactions tend to be resolved without physical conflict. But not always. Monumental battles can take place, and can lead to significant injuries such as amputation of limbs. If the body cavity is punctured, and water is allowed inside, peritonitis and septicaemia can be fatal. One of the main reasons for the bony armour along the back appears to be to prevent the teeth of other crocodiles penetrating the body cavity.

The power with which crocodiles can hit each other with their heads during conflict is quite remarkable and can rupture internal organs, causing death. When a crocodile grasps the limb of another, thrashes and rolls, that limb will be badly damaged or even torn off. In dense populations of Saltwater Crocodiles it is not unusual for 20 per cent or more of larger males to be missing limbs. The snout and jaws are other areas frequently punctured, broken or partially amputated in conflicts.

How do Crocodiles Mate?

*M*ale and female Saltwater Crocodiles spend much of the year in uneasy alliance, but normally separated from each other by visual or physical barriers, or by adopting different areas of a water body. Intolerance disappears when the wet season rains begin, and they lie side by side without conflict. Courtship between adult males, which often exceed 300–400kg, and the much smaller females, rarely reaching 100kg, is a subtle affair that involves a lot of side-by-side snout and body rubbing in the water.

Actual mating involves the male riding the female, clasping her with front and back feet and rolling his tail beneath hers so that the two cloacas come together, and the penis, normally hidden, enters the female's cloaca and delivers sperm.

During mating, the male and female do submerge, but it can all be done in shallow water, less than 1m deep. Freshwater Crocodiles mate in the same way at the end of the wet season when the waters begin to recede. During this period, the aggressive behaviours between individual males and females appear to be minimised.

Saltwater Crocodiles mate at the beginning of the wet season

Are Crocodiles Loyal to Their Mates?

*T*hanks to recent DNA investigations, the simple answer to the loyalty question among Saltwater Crocodiles in the wild is 'no'. Hatchlings from some single clutches from individual females were found to have different fathers. The sperm are in the female when ovulation occurs and so the yolk-filled ova are fertilised immediately. The female carries all the eggs inside her while the hard shell is formed on each egg, and the complete clutch is laid together in about half an hour. They have mated with multiple males prior to ovulation. The situation with Freshwater Crocodiles remains to be investigated, but is probably the same.

Dominance in Hatchlings

In captivity the effects of dominance are very obvious. In a small group of hatchlings, within the first two weeks a few individuals will start to dominate. When this occurs, the group's growth rate becomes bimodal, with one or two hatchlings growing exceptionally fast and the remainder much more slowly. By grading for size at an early age, submissive individuals can be given a chance to grow, but if dominated for a few weeks it can take months for their growth rate to recover. If dominant, aggressive hatchlings

Dominant males are continually contending with potential rivals

are isolated, however, they often cease feeding and seem to sulk. It is as though they need to be able to dominate to maintain the processes associated with exceptionally fast growth. Dominance appears to be hormonally influenced. It is not unusual among captive-raised hatchlings for

Fatal interaction: 4.5m male with a 2.5m intruder

dominant individuals to become light in colour relative to submissive ones, which darken. This does not mean, however, that large dark crocodiles in the wild are submissive: colouration in the wild is influenced by water clarity, age and substrate colour.

Dominance in Juveniles

In the mid-1970s, when the early population recovery of Saltwater Crocodiles in northern Australia was first studied, it soon became apparent that social interactions between juveniles around 1–1.5m long were seriously affecting the numbers of crocodiles retained in rivers. As described at the time, it was as though there were a certain number of 'slots' in a river for juveniles and, once these were filled, 'excess' juveniles had to move on. Dominance is exerted by being aggressive with others, by approaching and chasing away, by aggressive open-mouth approaches and rigid inflated displays, but rarely by combat itself.

   The juveniles driven out of the main river channels disperse into small creeks and swamps, or more commonly out onto the coast, where their fate is unclear. Some find their way into other rivers, but nowhere near enough to account for the numbers that leave. Some may head out to sea and be lost to marine predators such as sharks.

Growth rates are linked to dominance within a colony

Dominance in Fast-growing Adults

*A*s a generalisation, males grow faster than females, but this sex-specific difference is not strongly apparent during the first year. Between individuals, the differences in growth rate are profound. This may be partly explicable by genetic influences, but we do know that behavioural dominance is involved. In captivity, a dominant male can steam ahead and reach 3m in length and maturity in 6 years, when the average age to maturity for males in the wild is 16 years.

Freshwater Crocodile growth rates in the wild are also highly variable between individuals, and decline steadily with increasing size. Among mature males over 2m long, the growth rates of some individuals can suddenly increase dramatically, which is assumed to be linked to the attainment of dominance within a colony. The largest crocodiles of both species are not necessarily the oldest, but are almost certainly those which assumed dominance early in life, grew fast, and were able to maintain their position in the local hierarchy.

In captive colonies of adult male and female Saltwater Crocodiles, one male will normally assume dominance and grow more rapidly. If that individual is removed, within perhaps a week another male will take its position, to be replaced in turn by another if it is removed. It does not necessarily mean fighting to the death, although this occurs occasionally, but is more related to threat displays, with occasional contact, which potential rivals rapidly learn to counter with submissive behaviours and retreat.

Do Freshies and Salties Get Along?

*T*he core areas of distribution of the two species tend to be separated, sometimes by geographic barriers such as the Great Dividing Range in northern Queensland, but often by habitat characteristics that reflect their different lifestyles. Freshwater Crocodiles tend to live in the far upstream reaches of rivers, where flooding may be extreme in the wet season. This does not affect their ability to reproduce since they nest in the dry season, in hole-nests dug in the sand.

The core area for Saltwater Crocodiles is downstream swamps and rivers, with muddy rather than sandy banks. Their nesting strategy is restricted to the wet season. Their mound-nests of vegetation and soil keep the eggs above water level in modest flood situations, and the rains keep the mound damp so that the incubation environment remains humid.

The species cross into each other's core areas at times. Freshwater Crocodiles move into areas dominated by Saltwater Crocodiles, particularly during wet seasons when the volume of water moving downstream is greatest, and they can find themselves in saline waters as the dry season progresses. The numbers found in such situations are highest immediately after the wet season and decline during the dry season, assumed to be because of predation by Saltwater Crocodiles. Large Freshwater Crocodiles have also been reported to feed on small Saltwater Crocodiles if given the opportunity.

Saltwater Crocodiles can move hundreds of kilometres upstream into core areas for Freshwater Crocodiles, where a large specimen can dominate the local population, eating some and causing many to adopt shallow-water areas or spend a great deal of time on the bank.

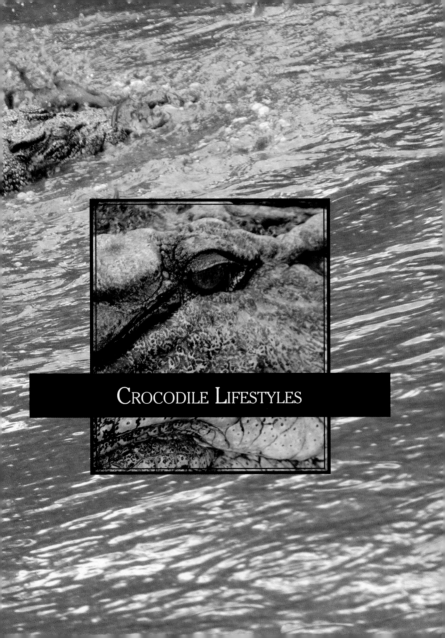

CROCODILE LIFESTYLES

How do Crocodiles Attack?

Crocodiles are agile hunters

*A*lthough all crocodiles are excellent 'sit and wait' predators, positioning themselves where prey are likely to bump into them in the water or come within striking distance on the bank, they also have remarkable hunting strategies. When their attention is attracted by movement on the bank or by vibrations such as splashing, they first orient their head toward the disturbance. Normally they slip below the surface and swim toward the disturbance, crossing rivers with remarkable precision even when the water is flowing at a few kilometres per hour, to emerge exactly where the disturbance was when they dived, followed by a rapid attack. If the prey has moved along the bank, the crocodile does not appear to be able to anticipate the lateral movement, and must emerge, reorient and try again. Waterbirds seem adept at moving fast enough along the bank to foil an attack—but not always.

Rushing Down Prey

Confronted with swimming prey in deeper water, such as rats, injured birds or even Water Buffalo, often the crocodile simply rushes it, swimming as fast as possible, head on the surface, twisting and turning as the prey changes direction, to grab it, drag it immediately below the surface, and either drown or crush it. They come back to the surface to eat.

Death Roll

In crocodile-based tourism, much is made of the legendary 'death roll'. This is for good reason. The way in which a crocodile can move its body relative to its head, and the strength of the skeletal elements joining the head and body, affords a remarkable mechanical advantage in overpowering prey larger than itself. The head of a crocodile is around 20 per cent of its body weight, and the jaws are lined with 60 to 70 interlocking teeth. The jaw muscles are designed to lock the jaws together with enormous power relative to the weak muscles associated with opening the mouth. In the

> So effective is the death roll manoeuvre that a fit 100kg person has great difficulty holding even a 10kg crocodile if it rolls in an attempt to escape.

context of attacking large prey, the prime function of the head is to attach itself to the prey and *hang on*. The body and tail are thrown into an explosive, rapid, rolling action, with the torque absorbed at the powerful junction between the crocodile's head and neck. The mechanical advantage is so strong that the prey animal is normally thrown off balance, rolled and disoriented, and thus more easily dragged into deeper water and drowned. If the prey is able to withstand the rolling action, the crocodile unrolls its body, and may thrash backwards, forwards and sideways before rolling again.

Crocodiles steal food from other predators

Do Crocodiles Stash Leftover Food?

*T*he idea that crocodiles hide large prey items in caches beneath the water until they rot and can be eaten is accepted as true by many. In reality, little is known about this behaviour. While crocodiles do not need a lot of food to sustain themselves and have relatively small stomachs, they take prey items well beyond their ability to consume in one sitting. At the time of capture, many prey items are torn apart by thrashing or have bits torn off which are consumed on the spot. Efforts to hide the remainder seem likely, but this behaviour has not been well documented and may be difficult in habitats with smooth, muddy bottoms. Saltwater Crocodiles placing prey (eg snakes, turtles) on woody snags above the water's surface and taking prey (eg wallabies) onto land and returning for it later have been reported.

The other problem with the notion of caches is that when a carcass bloats, it floats. Whole communities of crocodiles will feed on a floating water buffalo carcass, where some degree of decomposition may soften the thick skin and help in separating the body into pieces. Carcasses cached below the surface would presumably attract a wide range of other potential prey, such as crabs and fish.

Can Crocodiles Find Their Way Home?

*I*t was long ago realised that when Saltwater Crocodiles caught in urban areas were relocated well away in the wild, there was a high probability that they would return to the same location to be caught yet again. In one experiment, 17 Freshwater Crocodiles from a single pool 75m long were caught and relocated 30km upstream to a much larger pool (180m long) containing other Freshwater Crocodiles. Despite hundreds of pools between the capture and release sites, within 14 months, 7 of them were recaptured in the original pool. This suggests considerable homing abilities, but how crocodiles navigate with such precision is unknown. At this point, it is unclear whether relocation stimulates increased movement which by chance results in some crocodiles 'finding' their original capture site, or whether they truly have the ability to set a course for 'home'.

Crocodiles moving overland to return to their territory are sometimes caught in bushfires

Why do Crocodiles Dive Underwater?

*T*he underwater activities of crocodiles are poorly understood, partly because many live in muddy waters where visibility is poor and they cannot be seen when they are underwater. There are, of course, spring-fed streams and rivers, and many documentaries include underwater footage of crocodiles swimming along the bottom, more often than not for short distances until they find weed beds or the like in which they can rest and hide. That is, they appear to use such underwater locations for refuge rather than as part of a normal activity cycle. Underwater holes in the bank are also used for refuge. Crocodiles in captivity will pack into such holes if they are available, to the point that their activity enlarges the holes.

Physiologically, crocodiles are well adapted for diving. The heart has unique adaptations for shunting blood away

When capturing very large crocodiles, the first priority is to prevent struggling. Once the crocodile is secure, flushing the excess carbon dioxide from the lungs may be needed to avoid death by acidosis. In most captures involving large crocodiles, immobilising drugs are used at the earliest opportunity to prevent struggling.

from the lungs during dives. Crocodiles go through extreme bradycardia when they dive, the heart rate slowing from around 30 beats per minute when on the surface to 1–2 beats per minute. Depending on the degree of activity before a dive, body size, and perhaps body temperature and water temperature, a crocodile can stay beneath the surface without breathing for more than one hour. The question as to how deep crocodiles can dive has never been resolved, partly because they rarely live in deep waters. They appear to have no difficulty seeking refuge on the bottom in rivers 10–20m deep.

Do Crocodiles Get Exhausted?

The safe capture of large crocodiles is a challenge for authorities

*A*thletes pushing themselves to the limits of endurance in competitive events maximise the energy that can be produced through aerobic pathways (breathing), burning the oxygen they inhale during exertion. They also call on energy derived through anaerobic pathways which do not require oxygen, but which result in lactic acid levels building in the blood, and carbon dioxide in the lungs, creating an 'oxygen debt'. When the exertion is over, deep breathing repays this debt, flushing the excess carbon dioxide from the lungs and bringing blood acidity back to normal levels.

Crocodiles fighting, struggling with prey or trying to escape capture, are capable of an explosive switch from resting to maximum activity, an integral part of their evolutionary make-up. They usually do not need to struggle for long, but they do need maximum power and to be able to call on that power immediately. This is achieved almost exclusively through anaerobic pathways. A 3m-long crocodile can struggle intensely for about 15 minutes, by which time it is completely exhausted and has a very

Crocodiles need time to recover after capture

significant oxygen debt, with blood lactic acid levels induced through activity that are higher than recorded in all other animals. Blood pH levels decline to as low as 6.6, the most acidic blood measured in other animals without being lethal.

After perhaps 15 minutes recovery time, a crocodile can struggle again, but for less than a minute before exhaustion overcomes it once more. Very large Saltwater Crocodiles, more than 5m long and weighing over 600kg, can struggle for upwards of an hour.

By the time they are exhausted, however, serious physiological damage and death can result from blood acidosis.

Are Crocodiles Afraid of People?

Nest defence by females has increased since protection

*T*he effects of long-term hunting on the degree of wariness that crocodiles exhibit are poorly understood. Many Freshwater Crocodiles from the upper reaches of rivers in the Arnhem Land Plateau—where food is scarce and where Aboriginal people rarely ventured—although stunted in size, show little fear of people. They respond to any loud noise with an answering growl, approach canoes with aggressive displays, and sometimes engage in a tug-of-war with a fish on a line (without actually being caught on the hook), allowing themselves to be pulled right up onto the bank and even then not letting go of the fish. When crocodiles with such a limited history of contact with people are introduced into captivity, they settle down within days and start eating immediately.

These behaviours are not seen in Freshwater Crocodiles from areas with a long history of Aboriginal occupation or where there was intensive commercial hunting after 1950, so it seems that wariness has been selected in areas with a history of hunting. Hatchlings from eggs collected in different areas and placed in identical pens, side by side, can demonstrate vastly different behaviours.

Hatchlings from some areas are extremely wary and opt to remain hidden if there is any human disturbance, whereas others readily come up and feed together, despite people being present.

Immediately after protection, virtually all adult Saltwater Crocodiles were wary, diving and hiding at the sound of people or boats. No wild females encountered in the 1970s ever defended their nests, which virtually all captive female crocodiles do. Nest defence in the wild started to return in the 1980s and is now reasonably widespread. In a wild crocodile population, being excessively wary is probably not normally conducive to fast growth or normal social interactions. But hunting is lethal and can obviously drive evolutionary selection at the fastest rate. Hunting of crocodiles by Aboriginal people for food had occurred for at least 30,000 years before commercial hunting began. Under intense hunting pressure, extreme wariness may have been the only trait dictating survival.

The often-heard comment that Saltwater Crocodiles are 'more cheeky' now than they were in the hunting period is almost certainly true, and may represent a combination of genetic and environmental factors.

It is probably much safer to have 'cheeky' crocodiles that can be easily seen than to have wary crocodiles whose presence is unknown because they are hidden.

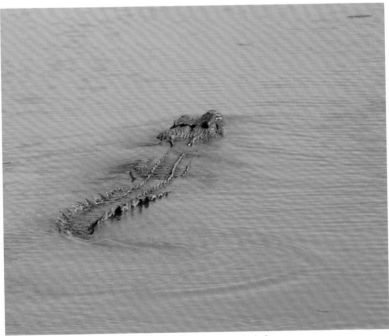

Some crocodiles avoid contact with people while others show little fear

CROCODILE NESTS, EGGS, EMBRYOS AND BABIES

What do Crocodile Eggs Look Like?

Saltwater Crocodile eggs in an opened grass mound

C rocodile eggs are white, hard-shelled, smooth and not unlike duck eggs. Alligator and caiman eggs are similar but are rough-surfaced. Unlike birds, which form individual eggs and lay them day after day until the clutch is complete, crocodiles, like turtles, keep the clutch inside their bodies and lay all the eggs at the one time. Egg size varies quite significantly. Among Australian Saltwater Crocodiles the average egg is 8cm long, 5cm wide and weighs 113g.

Hatchling size is dependent on egg size, with the average egg producing a hatchling 28cm long and weighing 71g. Before laying, the average adult female is about 2.7m long and weighs 80kg,. They carry about 6kg of eggs, or about 7.5 per cent of body weight. Australian Freshwater Crocodiles present a different picture. Using the McKinlay River population as an example, the average egg is 6.6cm long, 4.2cm wide and weighs 68g. The average hatchling is 24cm long and weighs 42g. The average adult female is about 1.7m long, weighs 14.4kg and carries 900g of eggs (13.2 eggs at 68g), or about 6.3 per cent of body weight.

Do Crocodiles Build Nests?

C rocodilians are divided into *hole-nesters*, which include the Australian Freshwater Crocodile, and *mound-nesters*, which include the Saltwater Crocodile. Freshwater Crocodiles nest in the dry season. Adult females with developing eggs begin digging test holes in sandbanks or a variety of other substrates, including gravel and humus, on occasion up to 100m from permanent water. The function of test holes is not well understood, but over a 3–4 week period, typically in August–September, all the females nest in a pulse. Digging a hole around 20cm deep, they deposit the typically small clutch of around 10–15 eggs in a half-hour period, then cover the hole and retreat to the water. Saltwater Crocodiles nest in the wet season, over a prolonged 6–7 month period. The females select secluded sites in vegetation 1–3m tall, in swamps, on floating mats of vegetation or on river banks, using feet and teeth to clear a site from 10 up to 50m². They pile vegetation, litter and often soil, into a mound averaging 53cm high and 1.6m base diameter. Egg-laying occurs almost exclusively at night. Excavating a 30cm diameter chamber in the mound with the hind feet, the female deposits the clutch of an average of 53 eggs. The top egg generally lies around 20cm below the surface. The chamber is covered and the female retreats to the water, typically within 10m.

Do Mothers Guard Their Nests?

Crocodiles are the only living reptiles that exhibit a high degree of parental care of hatchlings, although it appears likely that similar behaviour characterised some of the giant reptiles known from the fossil record. Female Saltwater Crocodiles often reside in wallows or water channels next to the nest, from where they can launch attacks on predators. Their goal seems to be to chase a predator away rather than eat it. Nest defence was rarely observed in the wild immediately after the hunting period, but has now become much more common. In captivity, virtually all female Saltwater Crocodiles defend their nests. Males are sometimes seen at nests, but it seems to be a matter of self-interest—the nest clearing may be a convenient secluded basking site. Among Freshwater Crocodiles, nest defence occurs rarely in the wild, but is common in captivity. Females excavate the nests at hatching time and care for the hatchlings.

A Saltwater Crocodile guarding its nest

How Long Before the Eggs Hatch?

A Freshwater Crocodile nest in the sand

*T*he driver of the incubation period is nest temperature, which tends to be more stable in the large mound-nests of Saltwater Crocodiles than in the shallow hole-nests of Freshwater Crocodiles. For both species, the average incubation period in the field is about 80–85 days, but varies greatly with prevailing ambient temperatures. In captivity, constant temperature gives highly predictable mean incubation times, which at 30°C and 33°C are 90 days and 68 days respectively for Freshwater Crocodiles, and 92 days and 75 days for Saltwater Crocodiles.

How is the Sex Determined?

*I*n the early 1980s scientists discovered that the sex of a developing crocodile embryo is determined by incubation temperature (TDSD) rather than sex chromosomes. This explained why sex ratios in the wild were often biased. In Saltwater Crocodiles, incubation at constant temperatures of 28–30°C gives 100 per cent females; at 31°C around 50 per cent males and 50 per cent females; at 32°C it gives 100 per cent males; but at 33–34°C swings back to 50–100 per cent females. A similar relationship occurs in the Freshwater Crocodile. The most plausible explanation for TDSD is that temperature affects growth rate, and TDSD allocates sex on the basis of growth potential. If the optimum temperature for producing a hatchling with the ability to grow fast is 32°C, and if temperatures higher or lower than this compromise growth potential, there are clearly advantages in a sex-determining mechanism that allocates maleness to those animals with the potential to grow fast. This implies that femaleness is the default sex, which makes sense in a crocodile context. Females whose growth is compromised will still mature and mate at some time, but males with compromised growth rates are unlikely to be able to compete.

How do Embryos Develop?

*U*nlike turtles and birds, in which there is limited embryological development in the eggs before laying, crocodile embryos develop considerably before laying. When the eggs are exposed to air in the nest, the embryo may only be small in size (about 5mm long), but already has a distinct head, heart, spinal column and muscle blocks. Dramatic changes occur immediately after laying in the allocation of

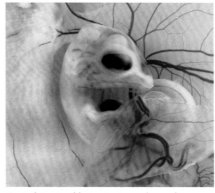

Sex is determined by temperature when embryos are about 35 days old

fluids within different compartments of the egg. Progress in this process is reflected in a chalky white band on the surface of the shell, which starts as a spot (exactly above the embryo), extends as a band, and by two-thirds of incubation extends around the whole egg. Inside the egg, this chalky white band is covered by a remarkable embryological structure, the allantois. This bag-like structure contains the waste products of the

growing embryo, and on the outside, pressed against the inner surface of the shell, is covered in blood vessels. These blood vessels also serve as the embryonic lung, exchanging oxygen and carbon dioxide through small pores in the shell.

A chalky white band indicates a live embryo

57

What are the Odds of Survival?

S urvival rates of crocodile eggs vary from site to site, and at any one site from year to year. The survival challenges for embryos are clearly monumental. The clutch of eggs sits in a mound of vegetation and dirt, or in a hole in the ground, but is otherwise unprotected from the elements. Within each egg is a sensitive and delicate embryo, complete with rations of food in the yolk and water in the albumen, changing in structure while it develops. A great deal can go wrong.

Among Freshwater Crocodile nests, predation by large varanid lizards (goannas) can reach remarkable proportions, exceeding 95 per cent at some sites. The general lack of nest defence by wild Freshwater Crocodiles may contribute to the loss. Varanid lizards use a keen sense of smell to locate freshly laid eggs. Predation on Saltwater Crocodile eggs is slight. Only if the eggs die and rot, and the female leaves the nest site, is there a rise in varanid predation. On the other hand, perhaps 70 per cent of all Saltwater Crocodile nests are lost to inundation. The embryos depend on being able to exchange oxygen and carbon dioxide through the pores in the shell, which is impossible if the eggs are submerged. Flooding can also be a problem for Freshwater Crocodiles because the dry-season nesting

period results in hatching at the start of the wet season. Some nests dug by Freshwater Crocodiles are so shallow that they overheat. The vegetation that Saltwater Crocodiles use to construct their nest mounds is sometimes energy rich, generating high levels of heat from decomposition. If nest temperatures reach 36–37°C, the embryos of both species can be killed, and those not killed typically have severe spinal abnormalities.

Flooding is the main cause of Saltwater Crocodile egg mortality

Saltwater Crocodiles hatching

How do Crocodiles Hatch?

*O*ne of the last steps before hatching is that the remainder of the yolk, the food supply for the developing embryo, is drawn inside the abdomen. This ensures that the new hatchling will have food sufficient to sustain itself for a few weeks.

The hatchling's movements within the egg weaken the connection between the shell membrane and shell, and it slices through the membrane with a tooth-like structure on the tip of its snout—the *caruncle*. Once through the membrane, the caruncle breaks the shell itself and the tip of the snout protrudes through the shell. The hatchling may remain in the egg with snout protruding for a few days, or burst out almost immediately. Regardless, it begins to make the hatchling call—a sort of *gnrrr, gnrrr*— within the nest. Mechanical or vocal disturbance at this time can stimulate other eggs to hatch. But here one of the great examples of parental care in reptiles is exhibited. The female crocodiles respond to the call by digging into the nest and releasing the hatchlings, often carrying them down to the water in their mouths.

Like Saltwater Crocodiles, Freshwater Crocodiles head for water as soon as they hatch

What are Crocodile Crèches?

Saltwater Crocodile hatchlings move immediately from the nest to the nearest water, or are carried there by the female, often forming a crèche, or pod, in the wallow next to the nest. The female remains with the hatchlings, and they may crawl up on her head and body to bask in the sun. The *gnrrr, gnrrr* hatchling sound plays a role in keeping the crèche together. A whole crèche on a riverbank can appear on the opposite bank, at least 50m away, indicating that the hatchlings can move as a unit. In captivity, a *pecking order* is established in a hatchling group within the first few weeks of life, and this may also occur in the wild. Individuals begin to drift away within two months, but they may join crèches further downstream, perhaps older or younger, and thus come under the guardianship of unrelated adult females.

Freshwater Crocodiles exhibit similar behaviour in the wild. Once in the water, especially in smaller billabongs, crèches coalesce and appear to come under the guard of a single adult female which, if her own nest was taken by predators, may be unrelated to any of them.

Surviving to One Year of Age

*H*atchling Saltwater and Freshwater Crocodiles, averaging 71g and 42g respectively, are almost perfect replicas of their parents. They are small and rather defenceless, and are assumed to be taken by a wide range of predators, particularly fish and birds, but possibly also varanid lizards, snakes, crabs and freshwater turtles, depending where they live. In one study in a tidal river, about 50 per cent of hatchlings were lost within the first year. With Saltwater Crocodiles at least, survival to one year of age is related to the number of hatchlings recruited to the population— *density-dependent survival.* In years with a lot of hatchlings, a relatively high proportion is lost relative to years in which there are few hatchlings. It is an important phenomenon allowing a depleted population to recover more rapidly. Among Freshwater Crocodiles, mortality in the McKinlay River area may exceed 95 per cent in the first year, mostly in the first two months after hatching. Some turtles are known to eat hatchlings and cannibalism may well be implicated in this high rate of hatchling mortality.

Surviving from 1 Year to 5 Years

*G*iven that it takes 12 to 16 years for crocodiles to reach maturity in the wild, juvenile survival rates ultimately dictate the rates at which depleted populations recover. In one large population of Freshwater Crocodiles, studied over a number of years, juvenile rates of survival appeared to average around 85 per cent each year. The reasons for the 15 per cent annual loss are largely unknown, although cannibalism and injuries inflicted through social interaction are probably involved.

Among Saltwater Crocodiles in tidal rivers, the proportion of 1-year-olds retained to the next year is highly correlated with the number of larger crocodiles in the same river, and cannibalism is the most likely reason. From 3 to 5 years, the numbers of juveniles retained in a river from year to year appear to depend on social 'exclusion': the rivers seem to have the capacity to sustain only a set number.

> Body weight increases exponentially with length, such that a 10cm increase in length in a 1m-long crocodile (body weight 2.5kg) adds 0.9kg, but a 10cm increase in length in a 5m-long crocodile (body weight 500kg) adds 34kg.

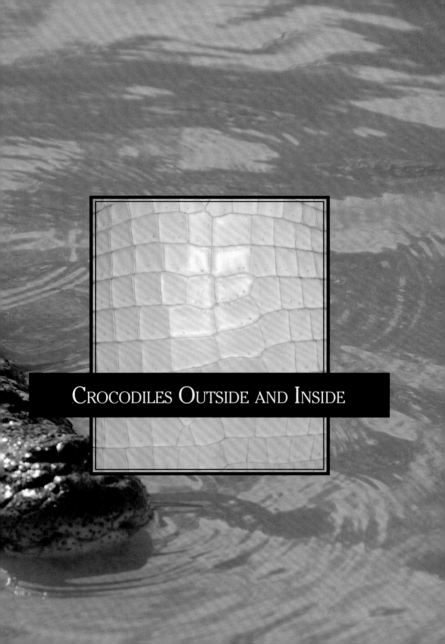

CROCODILES OUTSIDE AND INSIDE

How Big is a Crocodile's Tail?

The heavily muscled tail propels the crocodile along

*A*bout half the length of a crocodile is the tail. The main organ of propulsion, the tail is packed with muscle and serves as a site for fat storage in times of plenty. The length of the head, measured from the tip of the snout to the back of the cranial platform on the upper surface, is about one-seventh of the total length of a crocodile from the tip of the snout to the tip of the tail. In a 2m crocodile in good condition, the body weight is roughly subdivided into head 10 per cent, trunk 63 per cent and tail 27 per cent. Body weights are about 20 per cent heavier in captivity than they are in the wild, reflecting more food and larger fat deposits.

Why is Crocodile Skin so Thick?

*T*he skin of a crocodile comprises multiple layers of fibrous material that affords it great strength, both in the living animal and as cured leather. Crocodiles are often caught with small harpoon heads that utilise straightened fishing hooks with a 5mm wide barb to penetrate the skin. The full weight of the crocodile can be drawn to the surface without the skin tearing at the site of the small barb, demonstrating the immense strength of the skin. The surface of the skin is covered in scales, each with a thick protective outer layer made of keratin. The scales tend to be squarish on the belly and sides of the tail, and roundish on the sides of the body and the top surfaces. In

Bone strengthens the dorsal armour

both Australian species, each belly scale has a clearly defined pit which is highly innervated and appears to be a sensory organ. Along the back of the body, the scales contain *osteoderms*, large, thick, sculptured bone plates, comprising a bony armour that makes it very difficult for the teeth of other crocodiles to penetrate during conflict. Along the tail, the upper scales are converted to vertical fins that greatly increase the surface area. The dorsal scales all contain a rich blood supply, and during basking play an important role in trapping heat subsequently distributed to the inner body by the circulating blood. In the Freshwater Crocodile and most other crocodilians, small osteoderms form in many of the belly scales, giving them increased strength, but this does not occur in the Saltwater Crocodile. The number and configuration of scales is set permanently in the embryo and varies from species to species.

How Well do Crocodiles See?

Crocodiles can see colour

*C*rocodiles' eyes are adapted to their nocturnal and semi-aquatic lifestyle. They have upper and lower scaly eyelids and a more or less transparent inner third eyelid or *nictitating membrane* that moves horizontally across the eyeball. Underwater, the surface of the eyeball is protected by the nictitating membrane, through which light can penetrate, although the degree to which visual acuity is affected is unknown. The retina has rods and cones, which indicate that crocodiles can discern colour. In some captive environments, different coloured buckets are used to signal to the crocodiles whether they are going to be fed or their pen cleaned, and they alter their behaviour accordingly. The retina, as in many nocturnal animals, contains a layer of crystals that magnify the available light at night and in low light levels. Because of this, crocodile eyes shine red in the beam of a torch at night.

> Like the pupil of a cat, the crocodile pupil closes to a vertical slit during the day, restricting the amount of light that enters the eyeball, and opens completely at night.

What Can Crocodiles Hear?

*T*he ears are located at the back of the head on either side of the square *cranial platform*. The external ears are long flaps of tissue that fit tightly against the skull to form a watertight seal—they do not protrude like the ears of mammals. The inner ear is associated with a canal that runs from one side of the skull to the other, with the eardrums on either side. This arrangement is thought to be related to the crocodile's very acute ability to pinpoint the source of vibrations in the water.

Crocodile communications tend to be low-frequency growls in the air or low-frequency vibrations generated in the water by slapping the head on the surface or vibrating their sides. In cases such as the Northern Territory's famous 'Sweetheart', a large old crocodile which started attacking fishing boats at night, and in particular the propellers of outboard engines, it is thought that the animal's eyesight may have failed with age but its ability to receive and interpret vibrations had not. The low-frequency vibrations from a propeller are very similar to the low-frequency growls of a rival male, and so they are attacked. In the Sweetheart example, the crocodile tipped the boat over but remained fighting the boat while ignoring the fishermen who swam in the dark to the nearest shore...in record-breaking time!

Can They Sniff Out Prey?

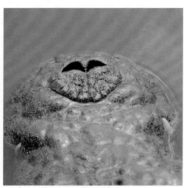
Nostrils on a raised nasal disc

*T*he nose of a crocodile is essentially the elongated snout. The crocodile breathes through two nostrils on the elevated dome on the snout tip, the *nasal disc*, when the mouth is underwater or closed. Within the snout are channels that take air through to the inside of the throat, next to the opening of the windpipe or *trachea*. Within the snout also are enlarged *olfactory chambers* where smell is sensed. The crocodile brain lies encased in bone beneath the square *cranial platform* on the back of the head, but the parts of the brain associated with smell, the *olfactory lobes*, are relatively large and extend well out in front of the brain next to the olfactory chambers. Crocodiles essentially have a *smell brain*, their sense of smell playing a major role in their daily lives. It enables them to locate the carcasses of dead animals at some distance from the water, and to locate prey such as flying foxes, which have a strong odour. Their sense of smell may also play a significant role in chemical communications, a subject yet to be investigated in any depth.

How Powerful are a Crocodile's Jaws?

Prying open a crocodile's jaws is no easy task

*T*he head of a crocodile is dominated by the flat upper surface, designed to present a low profile at the water surface, and the greatly elongated snout, which is in essence an elongated palate with the top jaws along its length. The lower jaws are equally elongated, are hinged at the back of the cranium but extend further posteriorly. The large, powerful muscles that operate the jaws are attached to the rear of each lower jaw at one end of the muscle bundle, and at the other end to the top of the skull through two openings, the *mandibular fenestra*. Opening the jaws can be achieved passively by tilting up the skull and upper jaw—the lower jaw falls open. Rubber bands are normally used to keep the jaws closed. In contrast, from the open position the jaws can close with enormous power, 2000–3000 pounds per square inch in larger crocodiles (9–10kN). Trying to open the jaws of even a small crocodile against the muscles keeping them closed requires significant effort with sturdy levers.

Only 25–35 per cent of the full tooth length is exposed. The long shaft of each tooth, firmly embedded in the jawbone, provides the strength needed to penetrate struggling prey or other crocodiles. With the exception of the oldest crocodiles, the teeth are replaceable throughout life.

How Many Teeth do Crocodiles Have?

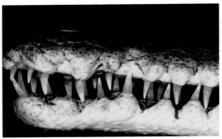

Freshwater Crocodile teeth

Saltwater Crocodiles on average have 64 teeth, 34 in the upper jaws and 30 in the lower jaws. Freshwater Crocodiles have more teeth, usually 70, with 38 in the upper jaws and 32 in the lower. A crocodile's teeth are all in place at the time of hatching, whereas an alligator's teeth develop afterward. The teeth of Freshwater Crocodiles are finer and sharper than those of Saltwater Crocodiles. In both species, the teeth in the front of the jaw tend to be long, conical and interlocked, designed for penetrating prey and holding them. The teeth in the very front of the lower jaw often penetrate completely through two holes in the upper jaw, creating an extremely strong locking mechanism. The back teeth are short, blunt and robust, designed for crushing prey once it has been caught and moved backwards in the mouth by rapid opening and closing of the jaws with the snout held high.

How Useful are their Legs and Feet?

The legs of a crocodile are small relative to the mass of body trunk and tail, which reflects in part that they are often simply tucked in beside the body when the animal is swimming with undulations of tail and body. The back legs are much more strongly constructed than the front legs and are able to lift and support the body mass when the crocodile high walks. The hind feet have four digits, three of which have

The hind feet have four digits

large claws, with strong skin webbing between the digits. The claws are not very sharp and are used mainly to dig into the substrate when climbing up a bank: not for tearing food apart or grasping prey. The hind feet are often used as underwater paddles to maintain postures in the water. The front feet are reasonably small—about 40 per cent of the mass of the hind feet. They have five digits, with slight webbing between them, and three of the digits have small claws.

How Fast do Crocodiles Grow?

Growth rates in wild crocodiles, in terms of increase in length per year, decline with increasing length of the crocodile. Yet because the animal's volume increases greatly as length increases, growth rates in body weight increase with increasing size. A small increase in length in a large crocodile involves a substantial increase in mass.

Within any one year, most growth occurs in the summer, particularly in the wet season when productivity of surrounding lands and waterways is maximised. Indeed, during the dry season many Freshwater Crocodiles not only do not grow, but also lose a great deal of weight, relying on fat reserves built up during the previous wet season. These variations in growth rate, as in trees, mean that growth rings are often laid down in the bones, with periods of rapid growth separated by arrest lines. Growth rings can be used in younger animals, which are still growing relatively fast, to give an indication of age. In older crocodiles whose growth has essentially ceased the rings are no longer of value for ageing. The use of growth rings can be confounded by remodelling of the inside of long bones as age progresses, or by the withdrawal of bone calcium for the formation of eggshells in females.

How do Crocodiles Eat Underwater?

Crocodiles have a fleshy, yellowish tongue that is fixed along its length between the lower jaws and acts more like a pad than a manipulating organ. Modified salivary glands in the tongue pump out excess salt, allowing survival in sea water. At the back of the throat, a large fleshy pad, the *palatal valve*, seals the throat, allowing the crocodile to hold a prey item in its open mouth underwater without water rushing down its throat.

What's Inside a Crocodile's Stomach?

*T*he oesophagus, leading from the mouth to the stomach, is thin-walled and very distensible—if a food parcel can fit in the back of the jaws, it seems to be able to pass all the way into the stomach. The stomach is a bag-like structure with the entry and exit points next to each other at one end, and usually contains a number of deliberately ingested stones. Food items stay in the highly acidic stomach until they are completely ground up and/or broken down by enzymes. Digestion is remarkably efficient: in the wild more than 80 per cent of what is eaten appears to be utilised, whereas in captivity food conversion rates of 25 per cent are commonly reported. The stomachs of many animals, including virtually all other reptiles, are designed to deal with a steady flow of food—but not the stomach of the crocodile, which is designed to extract the maximum amount of nutrition from food that is not necessarily available daily. In the wild, crocodile feeding is opportunistic, often a 'boom and bust' affair. Crocodiles can live for months without feeding.

The bag-like stomach retains any heavy and non-digestible items, and can sometimes be full of surprises. Miniature acrylic-covered electronic sensing devices fed to a crocodile can be recovered from its stomach, intact, after more than a year. If crocodiles feed on wild pigs, the pigs' bristles may form into hairballs up to 10cm in diameter, which are occasionally regurgitated.

Stones from the stomach of a 5.1m Saltwater Crocodile

A very common finding is bullets and lead shot: not an indication that the crocodiles themselves have been shot, but rather that they have eaten animals such as wild pig and waterfowl that have been shot and lost by hunters.

Crocodiles that have attacked people have been identified through items such as rings and watches found in the stomach. In India, where funeral ceremonies used to involve placing bodies in or near rivers, crocodile stomach contents revealed an array of metal bracelets and ornaments.

Do Crocodiles Get Sick?

*I*n the wild it is unusual to find animals that are obviously sick or diseased, and sick wild crocodiles are even less likely to be found. They have an ability to recover from horrific injuries, such as amputations, without the sterile conditions and medical treatment humans need. They can eat rotting carcasses without being compromised, partly because they have a powerful antibiotic substance in their blood that seems particularly well suited to fighting infections.

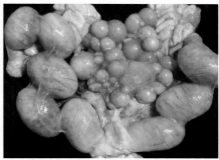

Ovaries and eggs in the oviducts

Do Males Look Different to Females?

*O*ther than large size, and the largest crocodiles are always males, there are no clear external indicators of whether a crocodile is male or female, for all reproductive apparatus is hidden within the body cavity. Ovaries and testes are located where they form in the embryo, next to the kidneys. The male's penis is hidden inside the butt of the tail, and is everted through the cloaca. During mating, the penis delivers sperm into the oviducts, where it is present to fertilise the ova when ovulation occurs.

Are Many Born With Birth Defects?

*W*hen one considers the highly controlled environment in which mammalian embryos develop, and that even minor irregularities can cause birth defects, it is truly remarkable that almost identical embryological processes occur in crocodile eggs with relatively few birth defects. Because their food supply is the yolk, rather than provided through a placenta, crocodile embryos are not as vulnerable to factors linked to the mother's diet and behaviour.

Do Crocodiles Ever Have Twins?

*C*rocodile eggs sometimes produce twins. Twins can come from the odd very large egg, when two yolks and two developing embryos have been pressed close together in the oviduct and packed into a single egg membrane and shell. They sometimes hatch and survive, but often one twin is large relative to the other, having dominated the space inside the egg, and both are smaller than the average hatchling from the average egg in the clutch. On other occasions twins come from normal-sized eggs with a single yolk, and within one clutch there may be a number of eggs containing sets of twins. Where they share the same yolk, which must be internalised prior to hatching, they do not survive.

Are They All the Same Colour?

*T*rue albino crocodiles, with no pigment and pink eyes, have rarely if ever been found, despite hundreds of thousands of wild and captive-laid eggs having been incubated and hatched. About 1 in 5000 hatchling Saltwater and Freshwater Crocodiles are considered *leucistic*, in which the background colouration and pattern lack intense pigment, so that they are extremely light in colour relative to the average animal. In the muddy tidal rivers of northern Australia that cross floodplains and contain high levels of suspended silt, resident juvenile Saltwater Crocodiles tend to be light and

A light-coloured Freshwater Crocodile hatchling

yellowish in colour. In clear freshwater areas, they tend to be a darker olive colour. Similarly with Freshwater Crocodiles: in muddy turbid waters they tend to be light in colour and very dark in clear, spring-fed waters, fully exposed to the sun. There seems to be a degree of colour adaptation to the amount of light to which they are exposed in their natural environments.

Do Crocodiles Get Hurt?

*M*ost injuries to wild crocodiles are inflicted by other crocodiles, either during conflict between rivals or attempts at cannibalism. Almost all Saltwater Crocodiles over 3m have scars or injuries. There are often puncture marks on the snout or injuries to the tip of the snout. Severe amputations of the snout are fatal, as are major breaks in the rear of the lower jaws, which can no longer function. Perhaps the most common injuries are mutilation of the feet and partial or complete amputations of fore and hind limbs. Many larger males and some adult females have one or more limbs amputated, but there is no real evidence to indicate how many crocodiles die from such injuries. Injuries to the tail tip are common. In Freshwater Crocodiles, the tail is a common site of rake marks obtained in the process of establishing dominance and territory. Both deep and shallow puncture marks and rake marks caused by the teeth are common on the belly surfaces of larger crocodiles. Sometimes hatchlings are injured by the sharp teeth of females when they are carried to the water.

Do Parasites Feed on Crocodiles?

A number of obvious parasites are associated with crocodiles. The most commonly detected is a nematode worm of the genus *Paratrichosoma*. The worms traverse the belly skin under the thick keratin layer. Leeches attached in the armpits or groin are common on Freshwater Crocodiles in some habitats, but tend to be small (1–2cm long). Barnacles are found on some Saltwater Crocodiles that live extensively in the sea. All crocodiles can become infected with an aberrant genus of worm-like arthropods, pentastomids, which migrate to the lungs and can be fatal. Microscopic flukes, emanating from freshwater snails, can also cause chronic illness and death.

Parasite trails in the skin

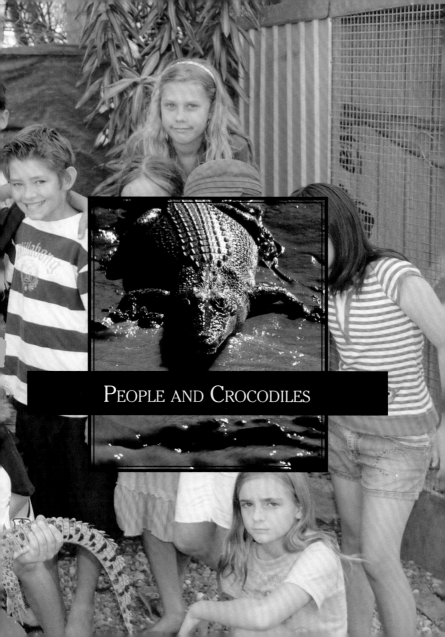

PEOPLE AND CROCODILES

Can People Live with Crocodiles?

Living with crocodiles requires education

*T*he degree to which people are prepared to coexist with wild animals, in the same habitats, involves a multitude of considerations. Of most concern is whether the wild animals have any significant impact on people or their livelihoods and, if they do, whether that impact is positive or negative. When wildlife is seen as a serious threat to human life, politicians rather than scientists make the final decisions. In this regard, Saltwater Crocodiles fall into the worst class of animal to live with because they attack and eat people and prey on domestic stock. They thus have an inherent *pest status*, and the human response to pests, in the household or in the wild, is normally to eradicate them. Laws alone are not particularly effective where lives are at risk. The conservation of crocodiles in northern Australia has depended on creating *positive incentives* for local communities to tolerate and welcome their presence, supported by education. The willingness to live with and tolerate crocodiles is inversely correlated with the length of time people and societies have had to contend with them. Where there have been no crocodiles in living memory, or for many generations, it is incredibly difficult if not impossible to reintroduce them. The longer the crocodiles have been gone, the more stories there are of their past dangerousness, and the harder it becomes to support reintroduction. People may be fascinated by television documentaries demonstrating what crocodiles are all about, but this also ensures they elect never to live with them. From a practical conservation viewpoint, when trying to reintroduce crocodiles into the wild, a sense of urgency must prevail. If it is not done quickly, while a culture of living with crocodiles exists, the opportunity may be lost forever.

Saltwater Crocodiles have a long history of preying on people

Are There Cultural Ties?

Where people do coexist with crocodiles, or have done so in the recent past, strong cultural and traditional links are apparent. Saltwater and Freshwater Crocodiles are involved in the Dreaming stories of the Aborigines of northern Australia, feature in songs, dance and paintings on both rock and bark, and serve as totems. The spirits of certain of the dead are believed to reside in some large crocodiles. Crocodile meat and eggs are still eaten across much of northern Australia as traditional bush foods. In parts of Papua New Guinea, initiation ceremonies for young men involve rows of cuts that subsequently scar in the shape of crocodile scales. The reverence attached to crocodiles in some societies may make predation on family members and livestock easier to bear. When crocodiles attack, they usually take their victim underwater, then resurface with the person in their jaws—a behaviour interpreted by some as the crocodile communicating with the victim's family, one last time.

Crocodiles are embodied in the cultures of many societies

What are Problem Crocodiles?

*I*n northern Australia, the authorities responsible for the conservation and management of crocodiles are also responsible for removing them when they spread into urban areas and along beaches used by people. In some locations, size and species are taken into account; in others, the presence of any crocodile is considered problematic. In Darwin, any crocodile that moves into the harbour and/or urban areas is removed. They used to be released into the wild, but because of their homing instincts, are now relocated to crocodile farms. In rural areas also, crocodiles that move into areas where they are a particular danger to farm workers or stock are sometimes removed.

Are Rogue Crocodiles Dangerous?

*R*ogue crocodiles are individuals in the wild that start behaving in ways that are inconsistent with 'normal' behaviour and which represent a danger to people. They are normally large older animals, and the cause of the problem may well be visual impairment with age.

Australia's most famous rogue crocodile was 'Sweetheart', a 5.1m-long male Saltwater Crocodile that started to attack fishing boats rather than people—a dominance rather than feeding behaviour. Another 5.2m-long crocodile in the Northern Territory's Wildman River began attacking fishing boats in 1985. In this case, it was attacking boats pulled up on the bank, biting into the warm cowling of the outboard engines.

It was assumed that this crocodile was mistaking the warm, protruding outboard as the head of a Water Buffalo, cow or pig, and that these attacks were aimed at feeding rather than dominance.

Problem crocodiles are now relocated to crocodile farms

Removing crocodiles from urban areas lessens the probability of attacks on people

Can Crocodiles be Kept as Pets?

*K*eeping crocodiles as pets has increased in popularity as captive-bred crocodiles have become more available, and as trends in the pet industry changed in the direction of keeping more exotic animals. A number of schools in northern Australia keep pet crocodiles—they are a focal point for education about crocodiles and help generate positive and responsible attitudes. Some keepers of pet crocodiles work closely with the animals, which become completely tame, and live like other household pets. To keep a crocodile requires permits in all Australian states and territories, and the animal must be obtained from a legal, licensed source. Keeping a crocodile requires serious consideration of how holding conditions may need to be modified and adapted as it grows ever larger. Small female Freshwater Crocodiles probably make the best pets in this regard, and male Saltwater Crocodiles the worst. The most common housing for small crocodiles is a large aquarium with temperature-controlled water and land areas but most crocodiles are returned to farms when they get too big.

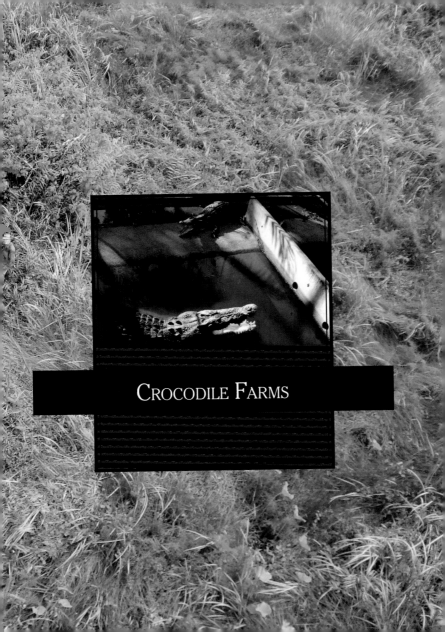

CROCODILE FARMS

Why are Crocodile Farms Useful?

O ver the last four decades, crocodile farms have been established throughout the tropical world. Some Australian facilities concentrate on the commercial production of crocodiles as a farm animal, but others cater to the increasing numbers of tourists visiting the north—people fascinated by crocodiles and wanting to learn more about them. Crocodile farms allow the public to get up close and personal with the animals, and provide venues that inform and help shape public opinion about the need to conserve crocodiles. Over and above tourism, the commercial production of crocodiles is a serious economic enterprise, to which Australian research has contributed significantly.

Where Were The First Farms?

I t is not that long ago that crocodiles were considered no more than dangerous pest species and their eradication a desirable outcome. Some of the first serious efforts to keep crocodiles in a farm environment were made in Cambodia in the 1940s and Thailand in the 1950s, where wild populations were going extinct through widespread persecution. Indeed, in Thailand some three crocodile species, among them the Saltwater Crocodile, are extinct in the wild.

In the 1960s, when international concerns about possible crocodile extinctions began to be voiced, conservationists turned to these pioneering farming ventures for assistance and guidance. They were seen as a way of producing crocodiles for restocking severely depleted wild populations, and as a means of supplying the market with skins without having to hunt wild crocodiles. Pioneering crocodile farming operations, often government-owned or supported, were established in many countries. One of the first, in 1969, was a government-funded establishment on Aboriginal lands at Edward River, in northwest Queensland. There are now crocodiles on farms around the world that are 5 to 10 generations captive-bred and raised. Their management is treated much like that of any other domestic farm animal and is increasingly supervised by Primary Production Departments rather than Wildlife Departments.

How is Crocodile Trade Regulated?

*I*n 1973, the Convention on International Trade in Endangered Species of Wild Fauna and Flora (CITES) was agreed; it came into force in 1975. At that time the fashion industry's demand for wildlife products was stimulating unsustainable harvesting in many places. Serious declines in the wild populations of numerous species were occurring, often in countries which had a poor capacity to manage

Crocodile farms played an important role in the first conservation efforts

their own resources. International trade was correctly identified as the link or gateway between supply and demand, and CITES was designed specifically to control that gateway—to open it and facilitate legal wildlife trade between nations where trade was sustainable and verifiable, and to close it where it was not.

Only experts can distinguish the skins and leather of the different crocodile species, and so all world crocodilians were listed on the Appendices of CITES. This meant international trade in wild skins for some species was banned, while for others, trade was only possible when it could be demonstrated that it was not detrimental to the survival of the species in the wild. Consistent with the thinking of the day, closed captive breeding establishments, such as crocodile farms, were considered good for conservation, and harvesting from the wild was considered bad. CITES made exemptions which allowed international trade in the most endangered species if the traded material was derived from animals bred in captivity. This stimulated significant investment and research into the production of crocodiles through captive breeding on farms because it seemed that in the future all trade in wildlife from the wild might be banned.

World crocodile skin production today is mainly from farms

Can Landowners Ranch Crocodiles?

*B*y the early 1980s, the conservation benefits of restricting trade in crocodile skins to commercial breeding was being questioned. Captive breeding establishments are ideally built next to a food supply rather than next to a wild crocodile habitat, and the economic benefits derived typically do not help the conservation of the species in the wild. A major problem in countries where captive breeding is the only form of production allowed occurs when the remaining wild animals are caught and shifted into captivity. In response to this, a new form of crocodile production, called *ranching*, was given special encouragement by CITES. Ranching allows landowners to harvest some wild eggs and/or juveniles and sell them to farms. The landowners are paid annually for their collections, and thus have a commercial incentive to value crocodiles and their habitats. Ranching puts real conservation value back on the wild populations of crocodiles and on the wetland habitats that support them.

Ranching with a Difference

Melacca Swamp, 45km east of Darwin, is a unique protected area. It has a core area of about 3.5km² of heavily vegetated spring-fed freshwater swamp which is home to a large and well-hidden Saltwater Crocodile population. The eggs from Melacca Swamp have been monitored and harvested annually as part of the Northern Territory's ranching program since 1980, providing the most comprehensive record of crocodile nesting in the wild, over time, for any site in Australia. The funds derived from selling the eggs more than compensates for the annual costs of managing the protected area. In this way, the costs of protecting all the fauna, flora and habitats within Melacca Swamp are internalised—this is wildlife protection paying its own way and being financially sustainable.

Do Crocodiles Breed Well in Captivity?

*D*ifferent housing and husbandry conditions are needed for Saltwater and Freshwater Crocodiles to breed reliably in captivity. This largely reflects differences in the degree to which the species will tolerate each other before, during and after the breeding season. In farming Saltwater Crocodiles there is a trend to breed with single pairs, with separate water bodies or the one water body divided by a partition, so the male and female do not need to see each other during periods when they elect to be alone. Early attempts to breed Saltwater Crocodiles in colonies, in semi-natural lagoon-type pens, largely failed. Males and females both engage in combat, which is often lethal, and the development of eggs and nesting appears to be inhibited by the presence of competing females. Freshwater Crocodiles are more tolerant of each other when living in groups, and are thus better suited to colonial living and captive breeding in larger lagoons.

Ranching puts another set of values on crocodile nesting habitats

How are Young Crocodiles Cared For?

*I*ncubation techniques for crocodile eggs vary from country to country and in part reflect the available technology, much of which has been pioneered in Australia. In some countries, the eggs are buried in moist sand, nest media or materials such as vermiculite within nest boxes and held in a room maintained at 32°C with high humidity. This produces mostly males if the eggs are collected when embryos are less than 30 days of age. Either sex can be produced by altering incubation temperature, but males grow faster than females and are thus preferred for commercial production. There is an increasing trend to incubate eggs on exposed racks, at 32°C and 99+ per cent relative humidity so that they can be easily inspected and progress monitored.

Hatchlings

The ease with which hatchlings can be raised in large numbers in artificial conditions varies from species to species: American Alligators, Siamese Crocodiles and Spectacled Caimans are three of the easiest. Their hatchlings begin feeding easily on a wide variety of foods and seem tolerant to a wide range of housing conditions in terms of density and space. Saltwater and Freshwater Crocodiles are two of the most difficult to raise in large numbers. They tend to be far more sensitive to foods and hatchlings from different clutches appear to prefer different foods. They are sensitive to the number kept in a pen together, to the availability of shelter, to noise, visual disturbance and a range of other factors.

Juveniles

Past the hatchling stage, both Saltwater and Freshwater Crocodiles are relatively easy to raise. They are highly resistant to disease and survival rates in captivity are usually very high. To grow at a reasonable rate, they need temperatures at which they can raise their own body temperature to 30–32°C. A wide range of pen designs is used successfully for raising juveniles. Again, density is important: if densities are too high, average growth rate declines, if too low, variations in growth rates increase, and with that variation comes dominance of larger juveniles over smaller ones, which results in the larger ones growing faster at the expense of the smaller ones.

What Kind of Crocodile Skin is Best?

*T*he skin of the crocodile rather than the meat is the primary market product. The most favoured type of skin is the *belly skin*, which from Saltwater Crocodiles is used almost exclusively for the manufacture of handbags. In times gone by, the majority of crocodile-skin handbags were dyed black, which hid small blemishes or bite marks. Over the past few decades, however, crocodile-skin handbags have been produced in a wide range of lighter colours in which any imperfection is obvious. To meet the demand for high-quality skins, crocodile

Crocodile abattoirs meet high standards

farmers have increasingly been using unitised pens, so that individual crocodiles are protected from dominant animals, and their skins are thus free of bite marks. The crocodiles learn to own and dominate their pens, and are accordingly less stressed.

When about 1.5–2m long, most farmed crocodiles, like other domestic animals, end up in the abattoir. Great care is taken in the skinning process because a single nick in the belly skin can halve its value. The skin is typically cleaned and packed in salt or brine to preserve it and kill any bacteria prior to tanning. The meat is the most important by-product.

What do Farmed Crocodiles Eat?

*O*ne of the most common crocodile foods is waste chicken meat but, depending on the location of the farm relative to the location of a food source, a variety of other meats is used, including fish, cattle, pigs, etc. To grow a crocodile from hatching to market size of around 1.5–2m and 20–25kg body weight requires about 100–150kg of food.

> Most crocodile meat produced in Australia is eaten in restaurants. It is white and tender without the strong flavour of many game animals, and is popular in tourist destinations.

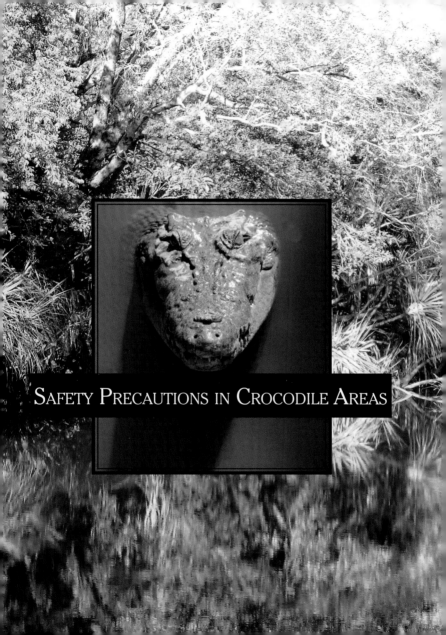

SAFETY PRECAUTIONS IN CROCODILE AREAS

Am I Likely to be Attacked?

> If people elect to swim in any northern Australian river with a high density of Saltwater Crocodiles, the chance of being attacked approaches 100 per cent.

*E*very country that encourages wildlife-based tourism and benefits from the economic activity associated with it has an unwritten obligation to keep tourists as safe as possible while allowing them the most exciting experiences possible. The crocodiles too (if they only knew it) have a vested interest in preventing injuries to tourists because such injuries stimulate calls to take action against them. Northern Australia has an excellent record of public safety, given the number of crocodiles in the wild, perhaps more than 100,000, and the number of visitors, exceeding 1 million annually. But it all depends on public education. In these times of enlightened environmentalism, it is tempting to use the relatively small number of fatalities due to crocodile attacks in Australia since protection in the early 1970s (21), as evidence that crocodiles are not as dangerous as they seem.

The dangers posed by Freshwater Crocodiles are reasonably minor, but not so with Saltwater Crocodiles. If people elect to swim in any northern Australian river with a high density of Saltwater Crocodiles, the chance of being attacked nears 100 per cent.

Crocodiles present real danger

Local Knowledge

Visitors venturing into crocodile areas should always seek, and heed, local knowledge about where crocodiles are present. Many access points to wetlands in northern Australia now carry signs warning the public that crocodiles reside there. But lack of signs does not imply safety for, sadly, they are sometimes removed by tourists as souvenirs. In the downstream tidal areas and associated freshwater swamps, core habitats for Saltwater Crocodiles, the assumption that crocodiles are present is wise. Further upstream, freshwater rivers, creeks and billabongs are usually core areas for Freshwater Crocodiles. It must also be remembered that Saltwater Crocodiles, generally large males, often move into these habitats—there is no easy way of being certain it is safe. Local knowledge is again important.

Swimming and snorkelling on the coast, where crocodiles are less common, also needs to be conducted cautiously unless the area is deemed safe by the regulatory authorities.

Floodplain billabongs are prime habitat for Saltwater Crocodiles

What Attracts Crocodiles?

*T*he kicking action of swimmers in the water is sensed by crocodiles from a long distance away. Some 62 per cent of fatal attacks have occurred on swimmers, and 38 per cent of these at night. Alcohol was involved in at least 43 per cent of fatal attacks. Even people familiar with the dangers of crocodiles can be prompted by alcohol to go for a night swim. Alcohol, swimming and crocodiles make a dangerous combination. If water activities seem essential, pick a very shallow area where crocodiles cannot approach underwater.

Crocodiles should not be underestimated

How Safe is Fishing From a Boat?

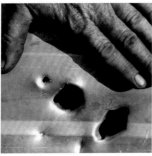

A crocodile's teeth marks in a boat

*F*ishing is one of the most popular recreational activities in northern Australia, and even in rivers densely populated by crocodiles, few people fishing from boats with outboard engines have ever had trouble—but canoes are dangerous. Their low profile, the splashing of paddles and movement close to the surface attract the attention of crocodiles. Best not to use canoes in any area where Saltwater Crocodiles reside.

Are Crocodiles Curious Creatures?

*C*rocodiles are often inquisitive. Fishing from a boat, day or night, you may suddenly find that a crocodile is approaching directly. Starting the engine and changing location is probably the best strategy; if this is not immediately possible, banging the water with an oar will normally frighten it away. At night, always take a torch and occasionally scan your surrounds for the red eye-shine of nearby crocodiles. Best not to let any crocodile get within a few metres of a boat.

What Other Precautions Should I take?

*I*t is dangerous to clean fish in the water, or to leave fish, animal carcasses or offal anywhere near a campsite. Crocodiles have a very acute sense of smell and are expert at locating dead animals. Never swim in deep water or sit on the edge adjacent to deep water. In areas where Saltwater Crocodiles may be present, it is unwise to camp close to water or on any gentle bank sloping down to water. Crocodiles have been known to crawl up into camps, attracted by the smells, sounds and activity. Attacks have been made on people sleeping in tents. Again, heeding local knowledge is one way of minimising risk.

Collecting Water

Conventional wisdom in crocodile country is not to collect water for tea or washing from the same site day after day. There may well be truth in this, because a crocodile's attention can be caught by the movement of people and/or the sounds of water entering a container. These patient predators have an astounding ability to learn. When collecting water, do so in shallow water. If you need to collect water from a deep spot, attach the

Be cautious near crocodile-infested waters

container to a long pole, stand as far back from the water as you can and keep your eyes trained on the surface. Bending down at the edge of deep water is dangerous.

Climbing Trees Overhanging Deep Water

It is sometimes tempting to climb a tree on the bank and move out on a sturdy limb overhanging the water—be cautious. Large crocodiles even some distance away can be attracted by the activity, swim underwater to the site and surface below the branch. With a powerful sweep of the tail, they can launch themselves to a height of 2m or more to attack what they see as prey. This is a common feeding behaviour.

Searching with a Spotlight or Torch

To maximise the chances of spotting a crocodile at night, hold the torch or spotlight just below eye-level and look along the beam as you scan from side to side. The best method is to pick a vantage point with the widest view of the water, approach quietly, wait two minutes without moving, then switch on your light source and scan rapidly for no more than 10 seconds. Wait a few minutes before you repeat the exercise.

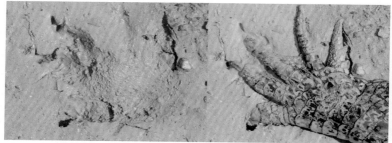

The front feet create a distinctive star-shaped track

Can Tracks be Measured?

*T*racks on the bank can indicate the presence of crocodiles. In the cooler months they normally crawl out of the water to bask, and the hind feet, with three clawed digits, may dig into a firm substrate as they heave themselves up, leaving a 3CLAW track. The width of the 3CLAW track, from the midpoints of the two outer claws, can be used to estimate the approximate total length of the crocodile. For example, if the width of two hind foot tracks between the three claws was 8 or 12cm, they would come from crocodiles about 2.3m and 3.4m long respectively.

In muddy substrates, the front feet leave a star-type track, with each of the 5 digits apparent. If the width of two front foot star tracks from the outside edge to the outside edge was 8 or 12cm, they would come from crocodiles about 1.8m and 2.8m long respectively.

The width of tracks from the rear feet can be used to estimate a crocodile's size

What if I Catch a Crocodile?

*I*t is not unusual to catch a crocodile on a fishing line. Freshwater Crocodiles (and possibly both species) sometimes take a baited hook on the bottom, and both will take lures. The hook normally snags in the mouth before the crocodile surfaces to swallow. The safest approach is to cut the line as close to the crocodile as possible. After a few days, the tissue surrounding the hook will soften and it will fall out, leaving no permanent damage. If the crocodile is small, it may be possible to catch it in a net or with a firm grip around the neck, and hold the head very tightly at the back of the jaws while the hook is removed with pliers. Opening the mouth of even a small crocodile can be a challenge, requiring the use of levers such as two screwdrivers. But be very cautious—a small crocodile can bite very hard. If it does latch onto a hand, it is important to prevent it from rolling.

Even small crocodiles have very powerful jaws ... best seen but not touched

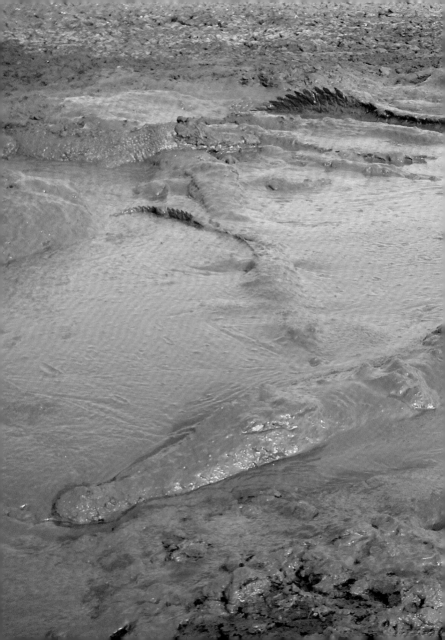

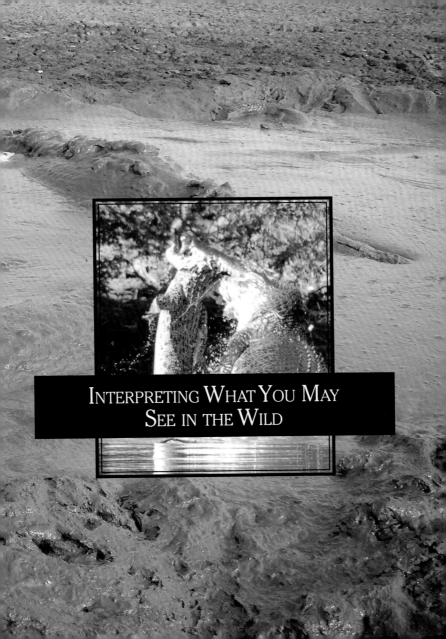

INTERPRETING WHAT YOU MAY
SEE IN THE WILD

Freshwater Crocodile basking on a bank	Saltwater Crocodile basking on the bank of a tidal river

Basking

Crocodiles control their body temperature by lying in the sun, ideally until body temperatures reach 30–32°C, then seeking shade or water to maintain the temperature or cool down. During the winter months in northern Australia (June and July) the maximum number of crocodiles will be seen basking on banks. In tidal areas, they are best seen at low tide, when the mud banks are exposed.

	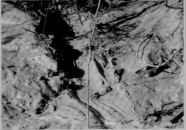
U-shaped track	Down track

Basking tracks

Some crocodiles are wary and will enter the water and submerge when they hear a boat coming. The shape of the basking tracks they leave tells you something of what they were doing. In the cooler months, the U-shaped tracks (left) are most common and show where a crocodile has crawled on the bank, basked in the sun, then retreated to the water. Slides coming out of vegetation or shade, often seen in the hotter months (from September to December), show where a crocodile has crawled or been lifted by the tide up the bank into a shaded site, then retreated to the water (right).

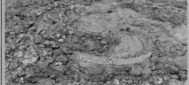

| Buried in mud | Saltwater Crocodile aestivating in mud |

Buried in mud

In the warmer months, in particular, Saltwater Crocodiles often bury in soft mud (left), with just the eyes and snout exposed. This appears to keep them warm but insulated from the high surface temperatures, and high water temperatures at the water's edge, while being well hidden from other crocodiles. They can become trapped in mud away from water, in which case they aestivate until wet season rains arrive.

| Saltwater Crocodiles with detritus on back | Saltwater Crocodiles with detritus on back |

Buried in swamps

At the end of the dry season, when temperatures are at their highest, Saltwater Crocodiles in shallow-water swamp habitats wriggle down in the substrate beneath the water. When they emerge, it is not unusual for the head and back to be covered in vegetation and mud, which stays in place when they swim slowly away or wait and watch what is happening. It is all about avoiding high surface water temperatures.

Saltwater Crocodile at water's edge	Freshwater Crocodile at water's edge

Water's edge

Crocodiles spend a great deal of their time in shallow water at the edge of the bank. In this position their feet rest on the substrate beneath the water, so they do not have to spend any energy countering water movements in tidal or flowing rivers. They can also catch small prey items that opportunistically move in the shallows along the bank, or on the bank itself. They are often in water too shallow for a large crocodile to approach them unnoticed.

Cruising Saltwater Crocodile	Cruising Freshwater Crocodile

Cruising

Crocodiles are often sighted simply cruising along a river on the surface, with the back exposed, the head sometimes lifted a little and the tail sweeping gently from side to side. The identity of some individuals is sometimes known to tour operators, who may know that this particular crocodile has a number of activity sites that it moves between, sometimes several kilometres apart. In other cases cruising crocodiles are dispersing, perhaps trying to locate a new area in which to settle.

| Large Saltwater Crocodile | Juvenile Saltwater Crocodile |

How big is that Saltwater Crocodile?

Although the head is about one-seventh of total length, and the distance between the head and the midpoint between the back legs is about half total length, it is often difficult to determine how long a crocodile is when it is seen in the wild. However, among males, the head becomes increasingly rugose (bumpy) with increasing age and size, such that old battlers (left) can be easily distinguished from younger pretenders (right), even if the same size.

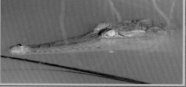

| Large Freshwater Crocodile | Small Freshwater Crocodile |

How big is that Freshwater Crocodile?

The length of the head is about one-seventh of total length, and the distance between the head and the midpoint between the back legs is about half total length. But it is still difficult to determine how long a crocodile is when it is seen in the wild. In Freshwater Crocodiles, the snout of large, old males (left) and females becomes more robust than in younger animals (right).

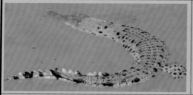

| Marked juvenile Saltwater Crocodile | Marked adult Saltwater Crocodile |

Look for missing tail scutes

Crocodile researchers long ago discovered that numbered tags are useful but tend to fall off over time. More permanent was a method of marking in which a sequence of raised vertical scutes on the tail was removed. As crocodiles can live for long periods, there are many crocodiles that have been marked this way in various research projects, and they are sometimes encountered in the wild.

| Saltwater Crocodiles repositioning a mudcrab | Crushing the mudcrab |

Feeding in the shallows

Depending on the time of year, juvenile crocodiles can often be encountered at the water's edge, feeding. Sometimes when a boat approaches and creates a small wave near them, it stimulates movement of small prey in the water, such as shrimps and prawns, beside the crocodile's head, and it will snap sideways into the water. If the crocodile catches something like a mudcrab, it will lift its head and move the prey back into its mouth for crushing.

Juvenile Saltwater Crocodile with large barramundi

Freshwater Crocodile with fish

Feeding on large prey

Despite crocodiles often being seen on television in the midst of a predatory attack on large game animals, in northern Australia this is rarely observed in the wild, partly because it occurs mainly at night and partly because crocodiles do not need to feed often. Sometimes a crocodile is seen with a food item in its mouth it cannot swallow easily and ocasionally cannibalism is witnessed.

Large Freshwater Crocodiles can dominate small Saltwater Crocodiles

An uneasy alliance exists between species

Uneasy alliance

Saltwater and Freshwater Crocodiles often have an uneasy alliance, because large Saltwater Crocodiles can eat smaller Freshwater Crocodiles and large Freshwater Crocodiles can eat smaller Saltwater Crocodiles. On occasion the two species can be seen together, although the communications going between them are hard to read.

Large Saltwater Crocodile eating a juvenile

Adult female with hatchlings

Cannibalism

Crocodiles feed on other crocodiles, which is one of the main factors controlling population growth and keeping the wild population at levels that the available resources can sustain. Historically, it was often reported that females ate their babies but it is now known that they are caring for them. Crocodiles are the only reptiles that exhibit parental care.

Saltwater Crocodile nest beside a tidal river

Saltwater Crocodile nest in a freshwater swamp

Nests

During the wet season in northern Australia, between November and April, Saltwater Crocodiles nest in a mound of vegetation and soil, which is often located on the river bank and can be seen from a boat. There may be wallows beside the nest, in which the adult female takes refuge, or she may use the river itself. If she has not abandoned the nest, her tracks between the nest and water may be obvious. Nests can also be seen in tours within freshwater swamp and billabong habitats, but they are usually better hidden among the vegetation. Although the last nests of a season tend to be laid in April or even May, they may be visible as distinct mounds for some months afterward.

| Colonial nest site for Freshwater Crocodiles | Single isolated Freshwater Crocodile nest site |

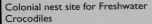

Nests

Most Freshwater Crocodiles nest between August and September. Where several female Freshwater Crocodiles use the same sandy bank beside the river, and nest in colonies, the bank can be churned up by 'test' nests (left) before the actual nests are laid. Other Freshwater Crocodiles nest in small solitary nests close to water (right). It is not unusual to see large varanid lizards, which are a serious predator of crocodile eggs, patrolling nesting banks.

| Saltwater Crocodile hatchlings at a recently hatched nest | Adult and hatchling Freshwater Crocodile |

Crèches

When hatching occurs, mostly between February and April with Saltwater Crocodiles, and in November–December with Freshwater Crocodiles, adult females near any hatched nests may be guarding a crèche of hatchlings. The size disparity between hatchlings and adults is enormous.

|  |  |
| Jumping Saltwater Crocodiles | Leaping Saltwater Crocodiles |

Jumping crocodiles

Crocodiles can feed on birds and bats that fly over the water, leaping up and snatching them from the air. They can also jump up to snatch animals out of branches overhanging the water. Many tour operations based on captive crocodiles demonstrate this activity by suspending food over the water, and in the Northern Territory tour operators have been allowed to feed wild crocodiles to show this behaviour. The wild crocodiles that learn to jump for food are very sensitive to the specific boats used by the operators and do not approach all boats expecting to be fed. Some crocodiles leap when startled.

|  |  |
| High walking Freshwater Crocodile | High walking Saltwater Crocodile |

High walking

All crocodiles have the ability to lift their body weight up on their four legs and slowly walk with the body mass held high. It is only possible where substrates are firm, and is far more commonly exhibited by Freshwater Crocodiles, which are more terrestrial than Saltwater Crocodiles and often have to overcome obstacles on the ground.

Galloping Freshwater Crocodile	Freshwater Crocodile seeking shade while walking overland

Terrestrial skills

When Freshwater Crocodiles basking on the bank retreat to the water, they often do so with a series of rapid bounds. When examined closely, this is a true gallop in which the front legs and hind legs move together. Again, this gait seems to be related to the more terrestrial skills of Freshwater Crocodiles, which often have to negotiate rocks and logs to get back to the water. It is the bound rather than the speed that may be advantageous. Freshwater Crocodiles walk long distances down dry riverbeds, seeking shade in overhands,

Dead Saltwater Crocodile	Dead Freshwater Crocodile with teeth punctures from a larger crocodile

Dead crocodiles

With crocodile populations recovered in many areas of northern Australia, it is not unusual to find dead specimens in the wild. Dead crocodiles in water sink below the surface; when they start to decompose, the gases inside the body cause them to float in two or three days, typically with the white belly up. Even a cursory examination is usually sufficient to see puncture marks from other crocodiles. However, with the spread of Cane Toads across northern Australia, which are toxic to crocodiles when eaten, there has been significant mortality of Freshwater Crocodiles.

Index

Further Reading
For an overview of the species in Australia:

Webb, G. and Manolis, C. (1989). *Crocodiles of Australia*. Reeds: Sydney. (Republished as *Australian Crocodiles* by New Holland Publishers, 1999).

More global treatments:

Ross, C.A. (ed) (1989) *Crocodiles and Alligators*. Weldon Owen: New York

Trutnau, L. and Sommerlad, R. (2006) *Crocodilians: Their Natural History and Captive Husbandry*. Edition Chimaira: Frankfurt am Main

For more technical information:

Grigg, G.C., Seebacher, F., and Franklin, C.E (eds) (2000) *Crocodilian Biology and Evolution*. Surrey Beatty & Sons: Sydney

Richardson, K., Manolis, C. and Webb, G. (2002). *Crocodiles: Inside and Out*. Surrey Beatty & Sons: Sydney

Webb, G.J.W., Manolis, S.C. and Whitehead, P.J. (eds) (1987). *Wildlife Management: Crocodiles and Alligators*. Surrey Beatty & Sons: Sydney

For husbandry/veterinary/trade:

Huchzermeyer, F.W. (2003) *Crocodiles: Biology, Husbandry and Diseases*. CABI Publishing: Cambridge MA

Fuchs, K. (2006) *The Crocodile Skin: Important Characteristics in Identifying Crocodilian Species*. Edition Chimaira: Frankfurt am Main

Operators for Crocodile Encounters

NORTHERN TERRITORY
Adelaide River Queen Cruises
Adelaide River Bridge
Arnhem Highway NT
Tel: (08) 8988 8144
e-mail: admin@ jumpingcrocodilecruises.com.au
Crocodiles in their natural habitat in a tidal river; feeding of wild crocodiles.

Cahill's Crossing
Kakadu National Park, NT
A public location in which large numbers of Saltwater Crocodiles in a tidal environment can be seen.

Crocodylus Park and Zoo
Grahame Webb and Charlie Manolis
815 McMillans Road
Darwin NT 0828
Tel: (08) 8922 4500

e-mail: info@crocodyluspark.com.au
Crocodile research and education centre; research museum one of the most comprehensive in the world; guided crocodile tours; Freshies and Salties of all sizes; American alligators; other animals.

Crocosaurus Cove

Corner Mitchell and Peel Streets
Darwin NT 0800
Tel: (08) 8981 7522
e-mail: info@croccove.com
Underwater viewing of crocodiles; other Australian reptiles; cinema and crocodile museum and displays.

Davidson's Arnhemland Safaris

Max and Philippa Davidson
Mt. Borradaile, Arnhem Land
PO Box 41905
Casuarina, NT 0811
Tel: (08) 8927 5240
e-mail: info@arnhemland-safaris.com
Saltwater Crocodiles in the wild; located within Arnhem Land; Aboriginal cultural links.

Katherine Gorge

(Nitmiluk National Park)
Katherine NT 0850
Freshwater crocodiles in upstream gorges; various boat cruises available.

Shady Camp

Mary River NT.
A public location in which very large numbers of Saltwater Crocodiles in both tidal and non-tidal environments can be seen.

Wetland Cruises

Ted Jackson
Corroboree Billabong
Off Arnhem Highway
Marrakai NT
Tel: 0427 678508
e-mail: jakkadu@hotmail.com
Guided boat tours at Corroboree Billabong in the Mary River; Freshwater and Saltwater Crocodiles; other wildlife.

Yellow Water Cruises

Kakadu National Park
Kakadu Highway NT 0886
Tel: (08) 8979 0145
e-mail: reservations@ gagudjulodgecooinda.com.au
Boat cruise showing Saltwater Crocodiles in freshwater habitat in the heart of Kakadu National Park.

QUEENSLAND
Australia Zoo

Steve Irwin Way
Beerwah Qld 4519.
Tel: (07) 5436 2000
e-mail: info@australiazoo.com.au
Home of the late Steve Irwin; crocodiles on display with educational show; other animals.

Crocodile Express

Dean and Anja
5 Stewart Street
Daintree Qld 4873
Tel: (07) 4098 6120
e-mail: info@daintreeconnection.com.au
River cruises in the Daintree River with Saltwater Crocodiles.

Daintree River Experience

Ian Worcester and Dawn Brown
Daintree River, North Queensland
Tel: (07) 4098 7480
e-mail: info@daintreecruises.com
River cruises in the Daintree River with Saltwater Crocodiles a special feature.

Hartley's Crocodile Adventures

Peter and Angela Freeman
Palm Cove Qld 4879
Tel: (07) 4055 3576
e-mail: sales@crocodileadventures.com
Wildlife sanctuary featuring Saltwater and Freshwater Crocodiles; crocodile attack and feeding show; boat cruise on Hartley's Lagoon; other animals.

Johnstone River Crocodile Park

Flying Fish Point Road
Innisfail Qld 4860
Tel: (07) 4061 1121
e-mail: crocodile@crocpark.com.au
Crocodiles and other wildlife on display; educational tours.

Koorana Crocodile Farm

John and Lillian Lever
65 Savages Road
Coowonga Qld 4702
Tel: (07) 4934 4749
e-mail: koorana1@iinet.net.au
One of the first crocodile farms in Australia; educational tours and shows.

WESTERN AUSTRALIA
Malcolm Douglas Broome Crocodile Park

Corner Cable Beach Road and Sanctuary Drive
Cable Beach
Broome WA 6725
Tel: (08) 9192 1489
First crocodile farm in Western Australia; educational tours.

Wyndham Crocodile Farm

Chris Lim
1 Barytes Road
Wyndham WA 6740
Tel: (08) 9161 1124
Crocodile farm with educational tours.